RAGS TO RAINBOWS

Miranda Innes

RAGS TO RAINBOWS

Traditional quilting, patchwork
and appliqué from around
the world

Projects made by Tina Ealovega
Project photography by Geoff Dann

C&B

CONCEIVED, EDITED AND DESIGNED BY
COLLINS & BROWN LIMITED

EDITORIAL DIRECTOR *Gabrielle Townsend*
EDITOR *Sarah Bloxham*
ART DIRECTOR *Roger Bristow*
DESIGNED BY *Carol McCleeve*

First published in Great Britain in 1992 by
Collins & Brown Limited
Mercury House
195 Knightsbridge
London SW7 1RE

British Library Cataloguing-in-Publication Data:
A catalogue record for this book
is available from the British Library

ISBN 1 85585 134 2 (hardback edition)
ISBN 1 85585 145 8 (paperback edition)

Filmset by Spectrum Typesetters, London
Reproduction by Colourscan, Singapore
Printed and bound in Italy

CONTENTS

INTRODUCTION

QUILTS ARE FASCINATING for all sorts of reasons — for one, they look wonderful, and warmth, comfort and cheer radiate from the kaleidoscope of scraps. They are an unpretentious art form and often the first of which we are aware: many a fortunate baby has been awakened to the beauty of pattern and colour through the quilt that formed the little world of its cradle.

When a child reaches the age for bed-time chatter, the quilt becomes a textbook of memory and anecdote. Every patch tells a story, and pieced 'schoolhouses' or appliquéd 'Sun-bonnet Sue' can start a train of association that will fire the imagination. Like a magic talisman, hiding under the quilt is strong protection against things that go bump in the night. It is a comforting association and is never forgotten.

The soothing magic of quilts goes back centuries, and the memories evoked by friendship, wedding or even the plainest utility quilts made from outworn clothes become part of family mythology. Generations later, there will be hazy and probably apocryphal stories recollecting who stitched what, and where the pieces came from.

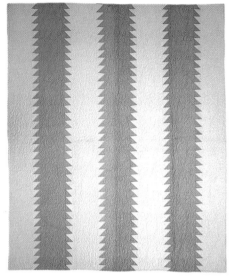

ABOVE: *Bearing the romantic title of 'Along the Lilac Path', this late nineteenth century Durham strippy is enlivened by a 'sawtooth' edging.*

ORIGINS: QUILTING

Quilting was developed centuries ago as a way of creating a thick warm textile cheaply. It probably originated in China and Egypt simultaneously — in the former as defence against bitter cold, in the latter as protection against unendurable heat. Remnants of quilted clothing and appliquéd heraldic banners survive from the eleventh century Crusades against the Infidel. In addition to warmth, the padding conferred some protection against arrows and cudgels. It was used as a substitute for armour by those who could not afford to encase themselves in metal, and as a soft and absorbent lining for those who could. The quilted red and blue velvet coat of the Black Prince, dating from before 1376, can still be seen in Canterbury Cathedral. Sometimes woven fabric was used, sometimes leather, and other, more unusual, substances also found their way into use as padding — the French

army of 1450 stipulated that thirty layers of linen should be sewn into deerskin for protective jackets, and the Elizabethan sage, Francis Bacon, recommended bran as a form of wadding.

Thick padding was necessary to give Elizabethan gowns the requisite stiffness, and Italian noblemen of the same era, like Titian's 'Ariosto', wore quilted jackets with voluminous sleeves. Eighteenth century British, European and American ladies shared a taste for full dresses with cut-away skirts revealing beautifully quilted silk and satin petticoats sensibly interlined with wool for warmth. In the nineteenth century the unfortunate inmates of hospitals and workhouses had to find less glamorous comfort from bedding composed of quilts stuffed with paper.

BEDDING

Quilted bedding was introduced to Europe by the Romans, who used a kind of stuffed sack or mattress, called a 'culcita'. It became an all-enveloping combined mattress and coverlet in medieval England and was referred to by the name of 'cowlte', from which the word 'quilt' derives. The earliest surviving example of quilted bedding is a funerary cloth which wrapped the body of a Scythian chieftain who died around the turn of the millennium. It is padded and quilted with a border of diamonds around a centre of spirals. Fighting animals in bright couching decorate the edges. Quilted bedding in Japan took the form of the 'yogi' quilt, the ultimate draught-stopper. A huge, thickly wadded version of the familiar kimono, it was filled with raw cotton and held together with unadorned straight lines of long white tacking stitches. It served both as mattress on the unforgiving tatami-matting floor and as coverlet.

In the fifteenth century, during a cold spell of several year's duration which froze the rivers Rhine, Rhone and Thames, the wealthy of Britain and Europe found warmth and comfort wrapped in quilted counterpoints (from the Latin 'culcita puncta' meaning 'stitched quilt') filled with wool, flock or down. By day, they countered the chill with quilted clothes, curtains and hangings. At the end of the

LEFT: *Finished in 1890, Miss Egglestone's Durham strippy is unusually ornate with five narrow patterned strips, and four broad diamond strips of muted cotton prints spiced with Turkey red. The whole thing is minutely quilted with hearts, chevrons, diamonds and cables.*

The quilt shows various embroidered scripture panels including:

"Come unto ME and I will give you REST"

"Whosoever will let him take the water of LIFE freely."

"Father I have sinned against heaven and in thy sight and am no more worthy to be called Thy son"

"Him that cometh unto ME I will in no wise cast out"

"Create in me a clean heart O God and renew a right spirit within me"

"The BLOOD of JESUS CHRIST cleanseth from all sin"

"In my Father's House are many mansions I go to prepare a place for you"

"Look unto ME and be ye saved"

"Yea though I walk through the valley of the shadow of death I will fear no evil"

sixteenth century, beds were equipped with 'a feather bedd, a bolster and a counterpoynte of tapistree'.

PATCHWORK

Patchwork was born of thrift, and the pieced and patched multi-coloured outfit known as 'motley' was the classic garb of the impoverished sixteenth century jester who would strut about the court in 'a pie-bald Livery of coarse Patches and borrowed shreds'. Harlequin had appeared on Italian, French and British stages since the late Middle Ages in his instantly recognizable suit of diamond patches. Patchwork clothing was also — like Joseph's coat of many colours — a sign of wealth and grandeur since, in the days before fabric printing and sophisticated dyes,

ABOVE: *'Hospital' or 'scripture' quilts were found in the dormitory of Durham Priory in 1446. This Victorian version is an unquilted 55 in/140 cm square whose somewhat chilling messages are immortalized in laundry ink on calico. Chintz patches add contrast and the back is a length of bright blue and white striped cotton.*

piecing was a simple way to make fabrics more ornate and colourful.

INDIAN PRINTS

Plain patchwork and quilting were part of everyday life in rural working England, but the passion for more ornate patchwork among the wealthy really began in the eighteenth century with the import of Indian chintzes.

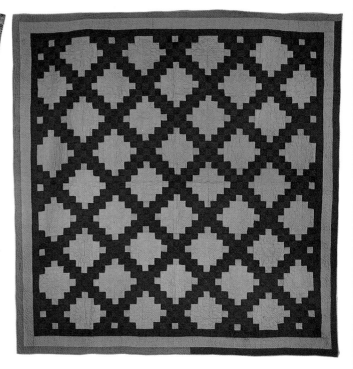

LEFT AND ABOVE: *Two faces of sophistication: an intricate Indian palampore (left), resplendent with its delicately printed tree of life and wide mitred border; a Mennonite Irish chain quilt in paintbox-bright colours (above), whose apparent naivety is a powerful statement of the simple beauty inherent in the plain and practical.*

They appeared in Great Britain shortly after the East India Trading Company was set up in 1600 (three years after the Dutch equivalent).

At first, trade was mainly in the area of spices. A few lengths of fabric found their way to Great Britain and excited great interest, but it was not until King Charles I officially sanctioned their import in 1635 that people could lay hands on them more easily. Their potential for quilts and hangings was immediately perceived, but initially the printed fabrics were not quite to the English taste. Consequently, botanical prints were sent to India as reference for the block-makers, colours were changed, and new patterns introduced — a few decades later, chintz was all the rage (until 1650 there were never more than 100 pieces of chintz imported at any one time, by 1660 there were never fewer than 1,400).

The influence of the Indian textile trade was immense, so much so that the import of printed cottons was banned in 1700. Home printing was forbidden in 1720; and it was not until 1774 that free trade was resumed. At the pinnacle of its dizzy popularity, chintz disappeared from the market, with the predictable result that it became more desirable than ever and was smuggled secretly into the country to be sold on the black market.

Increasing the impact of tiny pieces of the precious fabric became a challenge to which the needlewomen of the eighteenth century were more than equal. The exquisite Levens Hall patchwork — a finely worked set of bed-hangings made in 1708 — is the earliest surviving example. In this age of refinement the chintz patchwork quilt was born, and 'broderie perse' — in which small chintz motifs are appliquéd onto a plain ground — was invented to make the fabric go further and to emulate the laborious detail of crewel embroidery.

Pepys was a great fan of chintz and in 1663 bought his wife enough to line her study. For himself, he hired a chintz robe and had his portrait painted in it. It had become sufficiently rare and wonderful by 1732 for Alexander Pope to dream of it as a fitting winding sheet for a mythical hero: 'Let a charming chintz and Brussels lace wrap my cold limbs.' Six years before the import of chintz into England was allowed once more, two ladies were reported in the *Gentlemans' Magazine*, convicted of wearing chintz gowns. This constituted a mortal threat to the indigenous silk and wool industries, and they were severely chastised and fined £5.

The French repealed their ban on printed cotton fifteen years before the British, and an instant industry began with

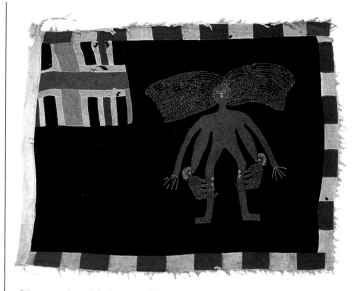

Christophe Philippe Oberkampf's print works at Jouy. Indian-style cottons were also printed in Provence and Marseilles ('les indiennes'), adding to the already crowded heady celebration of brilliant patterned cottons, which were finely quilted and made into clothing and thick furnishings designed to withstand the mistral.

In addition to chintz, the Indians manufactured 'palampores' — beautiful costly fabrics with a central printed motif surrounded by a wide, patterned mitred border. The colours and patterns were irresistibly rich and intricate and these too were smuggled to a voracious market in the British Isles and America via the Dutch, who did not have a trade ban, and made into quilts. Dutch museums abound in these sophisticated pæons to print.

ORIENTAL INFLUENCE

Following a different path, on the other side of the world, the Japanese were busy exploiting the peculiar ability of patchwork to achieve a whole greater than the sum of its parts. 'Yosegire' is a kind of crazy piecing using straight-edged scraps which they used to decorate clothing, hangings and screens, and which may have been the inspiration for crazy quilting in America and Europe following the great Japanese exhibition in the late nineteenth century in Boston. The women of Japan created magnificent robes for warlords and dignitaries composed of geometric pieces of imported Chinese silk brocade sewn together in strips. These not only looked beautiful, but conferred longevity on the wearer whose many glorious years would be reflected in the many sumptuous pieces of cloth that went into their construction.

Indigenous Japanese fabrics were always woven to the precise length and width required to make a kimono, according to a standard formula: two panels at the back, one and a half for each front, a width to make each sleeve, and one to bind the neck. To interfere with this perfectly evolved design would have been folly, so instead the Japanese invented a method of using large patches in the standard width as part of the traditional formula. There are two versions: 'katami-gawari', meaning 'half the body different', which uses two different fabrics; and 'dan-gawari', meaning 'stepwise different', using three. The effect is of disciplined richness: colours are limited and the excitement comes from the interaction of different patterns.

The Japanese military government imposed a total import ban in 1639, which obtained until 1853, and forbade the merchant classes from wearing luxury fabrics. As a result, the frustrated merchants developed an extraordinary mastery of indigo dyeing and printing using the very humble raw materials that were allowed. They perfected a style of fine decorative quilting called 'sashiko', which was initially a method of giving strength to the common loose-woven coarse fabric made from tree fibres that was the lot of the country-dweller. With characteristic style and taste, sashiko was refined into intricate webs of white stitching on indigo cotton and linen, and became part of the mystical

LEFT: *Harriet Powers' complex appliqué quilt, entitled 'The Creation of the Animals', is a justly renowned* tour de force *completed in 1898 despite poverty and relentless work on her farm in Athens, Georgia. It may have been inspired by the images appliquéd on to the Fante banners of West Africa.*

FAR LEFT AND BELOW LEFT: *Two heraldic banners, or Fante flags, from Ghana, combining cartoon commentary on local events with national flags and other decorative motifs.*

NOTE FOR AMERICAN READERS

In the course of reading this book, American readers will come across terms that will not be immediately familiar to them (e.g. 'wadding', for US 'batting'). In such cases they should refer to the Glossary of English/American Terms on page 128, where full explanation is given.

paraphernalia of the samurai warrior. The idea of 'hidden elegance' became enshrined in the Japanese aesthetic, referring to the clandestine wearing of forbidden garments beneath the dull decreed outer clothes; hence the predilection for layered clothing.

EUROPE AND AMERICA

The nineteenth century was the great quilt age in Europe and America — pieced block quilts were an American innovation, as was the radiant work of the Amish and Mennonite communities. In Great Britain, wholecloth quilts, medallion patches, all-over patches worked with paper templates, and strippy quilts were the most prevalent. Exuberant use was made of tailors' samples and cotton manufacturers' sprigged and floral scraps. It was a time of quilting-bees, parties and frolics, when the country population would gather together and make one or more quilts in an afternoon. These were sociable occasions, and welcomed in a rural community where the local church was often the only meeting place. They were a chance for women to meet away from the confines of the house, while still doing something 'useful'.

Quilting and other forms of craft were outlets for artistic expression that cut across social boundaries. Money, education and refinement are irrelevant where a pleasing

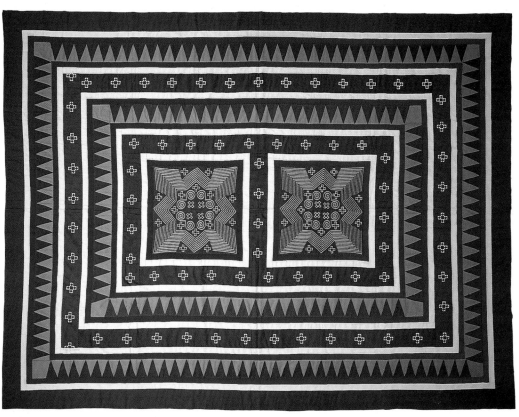

design is concerned. The disdained and maligned utility quilt made from old work-shirts can be quite as handsome as any fussy concatenation of thousands of minute postage stamps of dissonant silks stitched by ladies of leisure.

In the packaged, sanitized, standardized machine age in which we live, social divisions are thankfully less rigid, but individuality is still a rare and prized commodity. When so much of our lives is beyond our control and the family is

ABOVE AND BELOW LEFT: A vibrant parrot (below left), one of the favoured motifs of Kuna Indian molas, here intended for use on a blouse-front. The complex reverse appliqué technique is very similar to that used by the Hmong in Thailand to make rather more sober unquilted coverlets (above).

not always a rock-solid refuge against the world, there is a particular appeal in the good old-fashioned values embodied in a pieced quilt.

RIGHT AND ABOVE LEFT: *The stark elegance of a ceremonial jacket from Japan (above left), whose appliquéd double hatchet symbol broadcasts military prowess. Its silk brocade and fine workmanship are exquisite, in contrast to a rather more casual quilted cotton jacket from Persia (right), whose main charm lies in its skilful juxtaposition of two similar prints.*

AFRICAN PIECED QUILT

IN MANY PLACES around the world, weaving is done on a back-strap loom or a belt loom, producing long narrow strips of cloth which have to be stitched together along the selvedges to make fabric of usable width. The advantage to the weaver is usually that the whole contraption is basic, cheap and portable and can be worked on during odd moments. In West Africa, itinerant weavers have plied their trade for centuries, working out of doors in the dry season. Fragments of checked and striped indigo strip weaving identical to that woven today have been found and carbon-dated to the eleventh century. The looms are usually composed of sticks or wood, stones and string. With this primitive equipment, fabric of great sophistication and style is produced.

Cotton is the traditional fibre, with sheeps' wool, silk, camel and goat hair as alternatives. But times have changed, and West Africans now also relish the glamour and sparkle of man-made fibres such as rayon and lurex. Most cloth is white, often in combination with indigo. Natural shades of brown enrich the basic palette further,

and a variety of woven checks and stripes, ikat stripes and tapestry-weave chevrons serve as patterns. The weave of the cloth is sometimes dignified with a descriptive name, such as 'speckled indigo'; there are white weaves known as 'guinea fowl', 'cricket legs', 'albino maiden' and 'yam porridge which has red in it'. It is usually the men who weave prestige cloth on double-heddle looms. For many types of cloth, it takes a whole day to weave a single yard.

Simple geometric patterns are occasionally woven into the weft to represent combs, stools and other household objects. Diamonds, triangles, chevrons and ziggurats contribute to the richness of design — when these patterns are very elaborate they are given the title 'adwinasa', translated as 'fullness of ornament', or 'my skill is exhausted'. The resulting ribbons of material are pieced together in long continuous strips and are used to make voluminous robes for men, sarongs for women, blankets, turbans and headscarves, wall-hangings and hammocks.

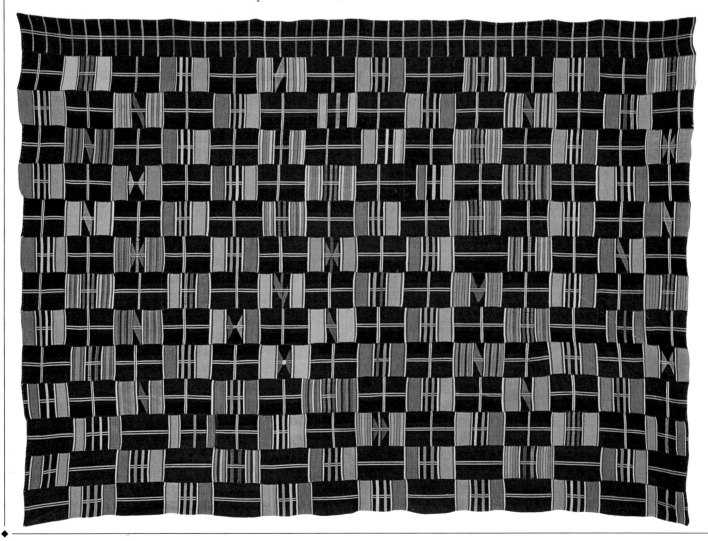

BELOW LEFT: *A vibrant partnership of colours in a cotton chequerboard all-purpose garment made from fabrics woven on a double-heddle loom by the Ewe, Ghana.*

RIGHT: *Close inspection reveals the fine weave, the subtle colours and the labour involved in making 4 in/ 10 cm wide strips of fabric into a continuous textile.*

BELOW: *The amount of material required for a finished Ewe cloth has to be carefully calculated before weaving so that there is enough but not too much of each pattern for the alternating blocks of colour.*

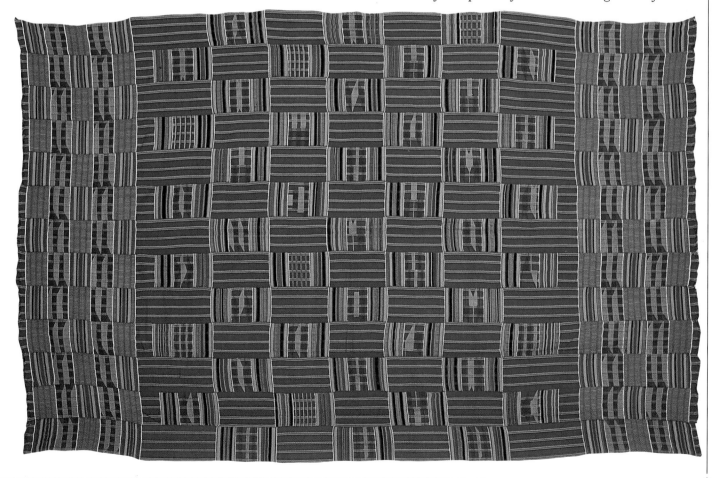

AFRICAN PIECED QUILT

A bold and sophisticated throw in a style which owes nothing to cautious dainty patchwork. Here exuberant stripes and brilliant colours are enhanced by a shiny satin weave. The inspiration comes straight from Ghanaian Asante textiles, producing a strong contemporary look, charged with the panache of its traditional West African origins.

WEST AFRICAN TEXTILES are an exciting marriage between the simplest technology and centuries of intuition and expertise. With the most basic looms, composed of sticks, stones and string, Ewe, Yoruba, Mende and Asante weavers produce fabrics whose mastery of woven design and colour is unequalled anywhere in the world.

The limitations of the looms are cheerfully exploited, and the narrow strips they produce are patterned and pieced together so that the whole emphatically exceeds the sum of its parts. The width of the strips may be as narrow as 1 in/25 mm or as wide as 30 in/76 cm. While natural fibres are traditional, the West Africans also admire the brightness and sheen of many man-made fibres.

The Asante have been weaving cotton and silk for at least three hundred years, and the skilful alternation of warp and weft stripes in narrow strips of fabric, produces a simple but dramatic design when sewn together that is easy and satisfying to reproduce in patchwork. In other areas, wide stripes of contrasting plain colours are joined together to make a bold chequerboard pattern.

Traditional dyes produced matt colour on uneven handspun fibres, and came from cassava roots (red), cola nut (brown), mango bark (beige); the ubiquitous blue of varying shades was extracted from indigofera leaves. The favourite colours used these days come from chemical dyes and have no truck with pallid pastels — bright stripes of primary red, gold, green and blue. These are sometimes given extra definition and brilliance against black, or slightly toned down by the calming effect of burnt sienna. All is put together with masterful and sure-handed sophistication.

--- SHOPPING LIST ---

Black and white striped satin fabric
36 in/90 cm wide: 3 yd/2 m 75cm

Satin fabrics 36 in/90 cm wide:
3 bright stripes 1 yd/90 cm each

Black satin ribbon (borders) 3 in/
75mm wide: 5¾ yd/5 m 25 cm

Black satin bias binding ¾ in/
20 mm wide: 5¾ yd/5m 25 cm

Plain calico (backing) 60 in/
150 cm wide: 1⅔ yd/1 m 50 cm

Cotton thread to match each
colour

THE PALETTE
One black and white, and three brightly coloured stripes.

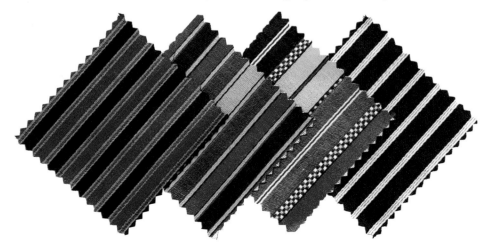

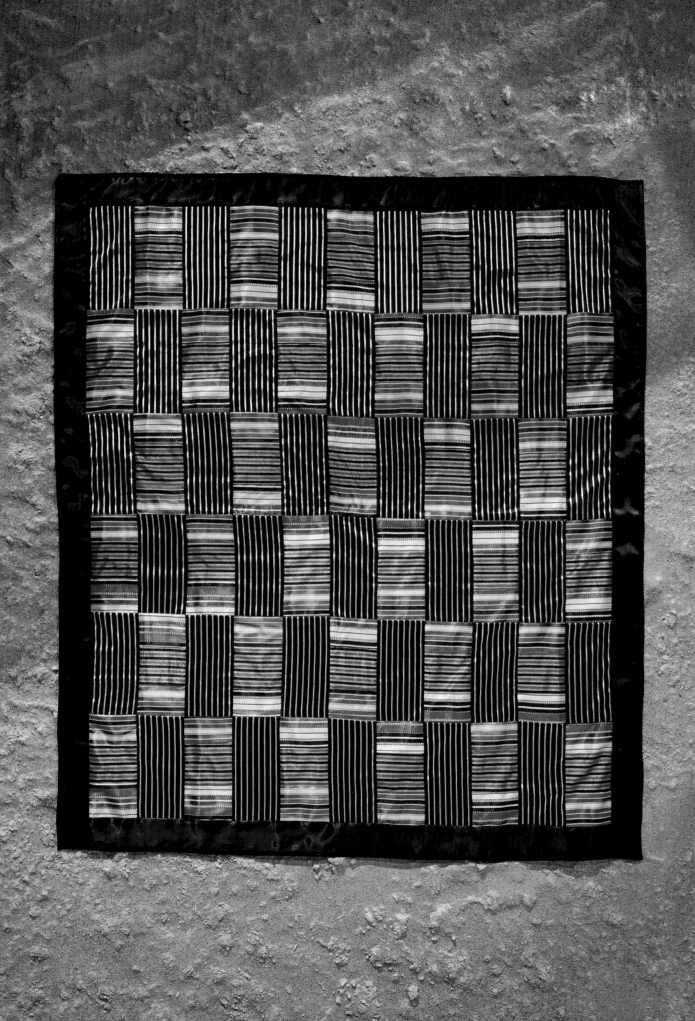

THE COMPONENTS

COLOURED PATCHES: 33, approx. 4½ × 8½ in/11.5 × 21.5 cm, made from strips of 3 different striped materials.

BLACK AND WHITE PATCHES: 33, cut to same size as coloured patches.

BORDER: 4 strips black satin ribbon approx. 3 in/ 75 mm wide, cut to size (top and bottom pieces to extend over side pieces).

Finished quilt measures approx. 46 × 52 in/117 × 132 cm.

BINDING: Commercially prepared black satin bias binding. Join and attach as on page 126.

MAKING THE QUILT

1 *Cut strips of coloured striped fabrics 2½ in/65 mm to 3½ in/90 mm wide, depending on the size of pattern repeat required.*

2 *Sew strips together lengthways using ¼ in/6 mm seam. Press seams so that they lie to one side.*

3 *Cut across stripes into pieces 4½ in/11.5 cm wide, making 33 pieces.*

4 From black and white fabric cut strips 4½ in/11.5 cm wide along stripes. Cut strips into 33 pieces the same length as the coloured pieces. Sew patches together to form rows of alternating coloured and black and white stripes.

5 Press seams outwards from coloured patches towards black and white striped pieces.

6 Sew rows together, being careful to match up seams (if you have been consistent in using a ¼ in/6 mm seam this will be easy; if not, you will have to stretch the shorter pieces slightly to align). Press well.

7 Sew on borders of black satin ribbon (see step 8 for Amish Cot Quilt on page 37).

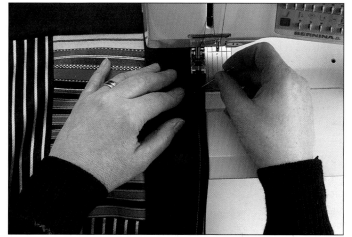

8 Cut calico for back slightly larger than top. Fix top to back with sticky wadding method (see page 125). Thread needle and wind bobbin to match top and back and stitch along seam lines on flatter side of seams (see page 125).

9 Attach black bias binding along whole of outside edge (see page 126).

AMERICAN LOG CABIN QUILT

THERE IS A mummified cat in the Egyptian sector of the British Museum, which has been preserved in linen bandages for 1,000 years or so. This fact in itself is astonishing, but what makes it more startling to a student of patchwork is the uncanny similarity of the binding to log cabin pieced work. Which just goes to show that the idea of creating a pattern with concentric strips of cloth around a central square is not a new one.

The subsequent history of log cabin patchwork is a matter of fierce debate, with British, Canadian, American and Swedish contenders for the title of originator. The Dutch had their own tradition and tended to use sober plain colours. An example exists of the technique in Britain dating back to the mid-seventeenth century in the form of a square silk perfume container. Further north, in the pine-forested expanses of North America and Scandinavia, there is certainly a visual connection, if not a practical one, between the construction of wooden houses built up layer by layer from sawn logs, and a textile augmented strip by strip from cut fabric — the inspiration for the design was to be seen all around in the architecture. Even the traditional red central square surrounded by light and dark could have derived from bright firelight casting warmth and shadows around a darkened timber-walled room.

The most common names have a self-explanatory rural or agricultural derivation: 'straight furrow', 'barn-raising', 'turning wheels', 'star', 'zig-zag', recalling the split-rail fence around the pioneer's patch, and 'windmill blades', familiar to the dust-plagued settlers of Texas who lived in troglodyte dug-outs and for whom the well and the windmill were necessities of life.

In the 1870s, following Abraham Lincoln's 'Log Cabin' presidential campaign, the pattern became wildly popular. As survival became less of a struggle and more sophisticated materials were recycled in quilters' scrap bags, bright variants on the old themes developed, using ever finer strips of costlier fabrics. Wool and linen gave way to cottons, silks, velvets, satins and ribbons robbed from millinery and fashionable clothing.

And, of course, the Amish achieved their usual magic with the simple formula, producing log cabin quilts in dashing primary colours, the unpatterned brightness of which makes the illusion of three dimensions all the stronger. The Mennonites enjoyed the same brilliant colours, with the risqué addition of small stripes and checks, while the Pennsylvania Dutch took over the technique and endowed it with every psychedelic shock that undiluted pink, yellow, green and scarlet, allied with stripes and spots, can effect.

LEFT: *A plain Mennonite version of log cabin in 'straight furrow' design, made around 1880 in Berks County, Pennsylvania. The simple colour scheme of earth and sky has a quiet serenity, and the backing of wool tweed embellished with chain quilting gives the finished quilt a satisfying weight.*

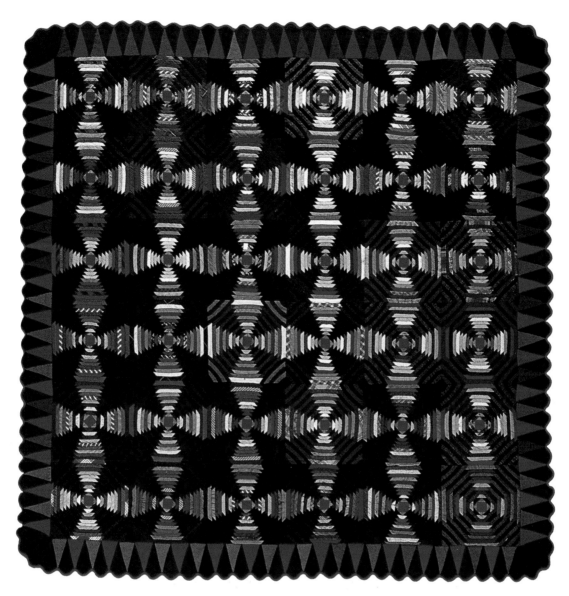

ABOVE: *Using characteristic dark and dramatic colours, this dazzling Amish quilt is pieced in a 'pineapple' design, symbolic of hospitality. It has a splendid border which echoes the main components of scarlet, royal blue and black, and has the additional complexity of a fine undulating binding.*

LEFT: *A quilt of rainbow silks made in 1914 by Constance Eriksson from Söder-Marjum, Sweden. The wide chevron border makes a dramatic frame, and the backing of bright yellow cotton is punctuated with royal blue pompoms teased out from the knotting threads.*

AMERICAN LOG CABIN QUILT

Tiny, precise prints in the colours of roses and jewels are used to make a log cabin quilt with a traditional air in a fraction of the traditional time. Light and dark can be arranged in different ways, but the hearthside glow of the red square at the heart of each block always acts as crisp and regular punctuation.

LOG CABIN IS an ancient quilt pattern with a decidedly down-home history in the United States, developed probably as a way to give a second life to unwieldy but warm fabrics salvaged from suits and coats. Fabrics of different weights could also be combined successfully. The basic technique evolved in the second half of the nineteenth century into a sophisticated, strangely three-dimensional design which ripples and undulates, jumps forward and recedes with the power of an optical illusion. Some of the 'pineapple' variants appear to have a life of their own, and the pattern seems to whirr in constant movement.

In Sweden, where log cabin quilts have also been made for at least two centuries, the style is more robust, and the use of good strong colours is more important than the passion for tiny strips.

One of the great advantages of log cabin patchwork is that it can be worked easily in cramped conditions as each block is made separately, and that when put together the finished article does not need to be quilted, thus obviating the need for a quilting frame. The strips are easy to measure and cut or tear to shape, and the quilt design adapts perfectly to

machine stitching — in all, the ideal pattern for those pressed for time and money.

It is also an adaptable quilt design, and can be made from different fabrics — silks and velvets hang well and give sumptuous richness; cottons are crisp and can emulate historic precedent with delicate chintzes or more humble prints and checks; wool challis and even linen in strong plain colours are authentic materials for a latterday Amish-inspired quilt. Narrow binding is one traditional finish to protect the edges. Amish quilts tend to have a wide border in two colours or pieced stripes, and more sophisticated versions of log cabin may continue the strip technique to make wide chevrons around the edges.

In the early pioneer days, when ingenuity and economy were all-important, bleached flour bags made cheap and hard-wearing backing cloths. The resulting cover was usually too bulky to quilt in fancy designs, and simple lines of stitching following the blocks, or knotted ties bonding front to back were the usual expedients. Many were left unquilted, since they were usually constructed on backing fabric and had comforting weight enough.

SHOPPING LIST

Cotton lawn 36 in/90 cm wide:
6 dark all-over prints ½ yd/ 45 cm each
6 light all-over prints ½ yd/ 45 cm each
Pre-shrunk colourfast cotton 36 in/90 cm wide:
Red ¼ yd/25 cm
Dark brown ½ yd/45 cm
Burgundy print 1 yd/90 cm
Burgundy 1 yd/90 cm
Pre-shrunk lightweight cotton (block backing) 36 in/90 cm wide: 1½ yd/1 m 40 cm
Pre-shrunk colourfast cotton (quilt backing) 45 in/115 wide: 4 yd/3 m 65 cm
4 oz Terylene wadding 60 in/ 150 cm wide: 2 yd/1 m 80 cm
2 oz Terylene wadding 60 in/ 150 cm wide: 2 yd/1 m 80 cm
Cotton thread to match each colour

THE PALETTE

Six dark- and six light-toned warm-coloured prints, a burgundy print, and plain red and dark brown.

THE COMPONENTS

*Finished quilt measures approx. 48 × 60 in/
122 × 152 cm.*

*'LOG CABINS': 12 blocks
light and dark strips
simultaneously seamed and
quilted concentrically around
the red 'hearth' piece.*

*BINDING: Burgundy strips
3 in/75 mm wide. Join and
prepare as on page 126.*

*SECOND BORDER:
4 strips burgundy print
approx. 4 in/10 cm wide (join
where necessary). The borders
are simultaneously seamed
and quilted on to long strips
of wadding, then cut to the
length and width of the
finished quilt, and sewn on.*

*FIRST BORDER: 4 strips dark
brown approx. 1½ in/40 mm wide
(join where necessary).*

MAKING THE QUILT

*1 Cut strips 1¾ in/45 mm wide from dark
and light lawn.*

*2 Separate strips and clip into light and
dark bunches using bulldog clips.*

*3 Cut 12 15 in/38 cm squares of plain
cotton and 4 oz wadding. Press cotton
diagonally to mark centres. Attach with
spray adhesive or pins to wadding. Cut 12
3 in/75 mm squares of red. Pin to centres.*

4 *Without removing from bulldog clip, lay a light-coloured strip face down on edge of red square. Sew to end of red square. Lift presser foot and draw out enough thread to turn work.*

5 *Cut strip even with edge of red square. Fold it out and pin open. Quilting and assembling happen simultaneously. Make a quarter turn.*

6 *Attach another light strip, sewing over previous strip. Make sure strips are parallel to edge of red square and all seams are ¼ in/6mm. Pull enough thread out to turn, cut off excess strip, and pin open.*

7 *Make a quarter turn and attach a dark strip carefully, exactly parallel to first, incorporating last light strip.*

8 *Continue to attach 2 light and 2 dark strips of random patterns, ensuring that they are exactly parallel, and similar strips do not juxtapose.*

9 *Completed square will have concentric strips of pattern around red centre and should measure 14¼ in/37 cm square. Pull it to shape and pin last strips outwards. Zig-zag edges and trim off excess wadding.*

10 *Lay blocks on floor to choose best assembly design. Seam them together just on inside of binding stitch, matching seams. Make 4 rows, then sew rows together.*

11 *Cut 4 strips wadding 5 in/13 cm wide, 4 strips burgundy print 4 in/10 cm wide, and 4 strips brown 1½ in/40 mm wide, all 54 in/140 cm long. Zig-zag brown strips to wadding.*

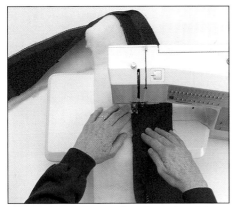

12 *Sew 2 burgundy print strips right sides together to left side of brown strips, stitching through wadding. Seam forms a quilting line. Open out over wadding and zig-zag raw left-hand edge of wadding. Sew borders to either side of quilt.*

13 *Cut remaining burgundy print pieces the distance between brown strips on attached borders plus ½ in/13 mm. Sew strips of brown and burgundy print to each end. Line up brown strips, trim and sew on borders.*

14 *Cut backing and make 'quilt sandwich' around 2 oz wadding using sticky wadding method (see page 125). Tack around edge. Hand-quilt along borders and between squares. Trim edges and attach binding (see page 126).*

AMERICAN WINDMILL QUILT

◆

T THEIR MOST basic, the windmill variants in patchwork are just one stage beyond simple squares, but the effect is dynamic and very different. For young girls beginning their patchwork careers, squares and rectangles came first because they were economical to measure and cut, and easy to sew. Triangles followed, made slightly more demanding by their bias edge which needs careful handling and is likely to split if stretched.

The essential component of the windmill design — the triangle — comes up in many different guises and forms as part of many different patchwork patterns, from bone simple woollen utility quilts composed entirely of triangles in just two contrasting colours, to decorative borders on the complex and sophisticated chintz medallion quilts typical of the late eighteenth and early nineteenth centuries.

In the British Isles, this pieced style was particularly popular in South Wales and the north of England, where it gave rise to more complex interchange patterns with such names as 'cotton-reel' and 'pinwheel'. In the United States, 'robbing Peter to pay Paul' is the common and descriptive name, along with the favoured 'baskets' (a beloved wedding-quilt motif, signifying well-being and plenty) and 'pine tree' designs. In Holland, windmills feature on brightly coloured quilts made from combinations of checks and chintzes often on a plain calico ground — see page 116 for examples. In Scandinavia the tradition is more humble though equally colourful, and the familiar triangles appear on utility quilts made from homespun checked woollens. In India, windmills spin in the bold colours of spices and olive green — turn to the Pakistani Tasselled Quilt project on page 98 for examples of quilts worked in this traditional palette.

RIGHT: *Dark colours in a twentieth century diamond-quilted medallion patchwork quilt, whose sobriety is enlivened by border strips of red and white checks enclosing bands of 'hourglass' patch squares and 'wild goose chase' triangles.*

RIGHT: *A medallion quilt from Dundee dating from about 1910. The 'wild goose chase' borders give an optical illusion of movement, and the design is made even busier by the contrariness of the black and white arrows and the substitution of a different red and white print in the border.*

BELOW RIGHT: *High drama and utter simplicity in a woollen twill quilt of navy and scarlet windmills made in Northern Ireland in the nineteenth century. A blanket serves as interlining and the quilt has the narrowest blue braid border and a startling paisley backing.*

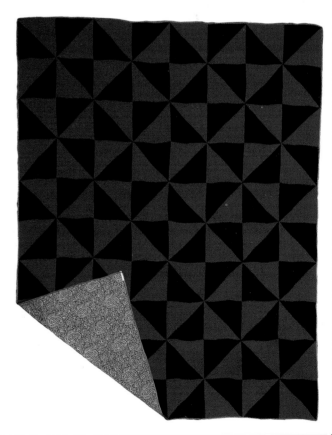

ABOVE: *An Irish quilt composed of navy and white windmills with an unusual ruffled border, held together with the plainest possible diamond quilting.*

AMERICAN WINDMILL QUILT

One of the many old-fashioned variants on the windmill theme, here the sails are put together from tiny prints in red and navy, against a background splattered with lighter flowers, to form a cot quilt busy enough to keep any self-respecting baby occupied for hours. A delicately patterned lining and lightweight wadding make a quilt that will improve with washing.

PATCHWORK DESIGNS CONSISTING of triangles, squares and rectangles are easy to work out and simple to sew. 'Flying geese', 'sawtooth', 'baskets', 'Yankee puzzle', and 'variable star' are all elaborations on the straightforward theme of a right-angled triangle. It obligingly makes a square when joined along the bias edge to an identical-shaped piece, and lends itself ideally to the quick and accurate RIT (Right-angled Isosceles Triangle) square method of machine quilting. Strips or borders made in this way enliven a more basic design of blocks, and were often used to make jagged and emphatic frames around medallion quilts.

Blocks and strips are satisfying to do, as they are speedy and can be adapted and experimented with to make dramatic patterns which grow as you sew. As with any repeating geometric design, accuracy in sewing and cutting is essential.

Also, as is so often the case with patchwork, complexity does not necessarily make for a more stylish quilt, and 'flying geese', the most basic permutation

of triangles and strips, can be unbeatably crisp and elegant. Various combinations of the simple elements — the square windmill block, right-angled triangle arrowhead, and serrated sawtooth edge, all based on triangle repeats — can be used in a variety of ways. There is a tradition of surrounding the initial motif in a medallion quilt, which might itself be made of harlequin diamonds, with lively concentric strips of 'flying geese'. A jagged edging of triangles can be used to feather the edge of complex shapes, like stars (also made up of triangular components), or to embellish the simple strips of colour in a strippy quilt. The strippy pieces themselves can also be complex combinations of squares and triangles. The quilt may be composed entirely of triangles, as in the restless lattice design called 'ocean waves', or tiny triangles may be minutely sewn together into larger triangles to form busy multi-coloured pennants on a plain ground. As always in patchwork, the whole is much greater than the sum of its parts.

SHOPPING LIST

The prints in each colour should be near in tone but different enough to contrast slightly.

Cotton fabric 45 in/115 cm wide:

3 different tiny navy prints ½ yd/ 45 cm each

4 different tiny red prints ½ yd/ 45 cm each

4 different light-toned prints ½ yd/45 cm each

Plain navy ¼ yd/25 cm

Light-toned cotton print (backing) 45 in/115 cm wide: 1¼ yd/ 1 m 15 cm

4 oz Terylene wadding 60 in/ 150 cm wide: 1¼ yd/1 m 15 cm

Bondaweb: 12 in/30 cm

Toning cotton thread and/or invisible nylon thread

THE PALETTE
Three navy prints, four red prints, four light-toned prints and plain navy.

THE COMPONENTS

Use RIT square
templates on page 124.

RED WINDMILLS:
6, made from 24 no. 2
RIT squares in light
and dark red prints.

BLUE WINDMILLS:
6, made from 24 no. 2
RIT squares in light and
dark blue prints.

HOURGLASS PATCH
SQUARES: 62 no. 3 RIT
squares made from light and
dark blue and red prints.

RED SQUARES: 6 no. 1
RIT squares made from red
print, each with a smaller
square of light print
appliquéd to centre.

Finished quilt measures approx.
34 × 41 in/86 × 104 cm.

FIRST BORDER: 4 strips
plain navy approx. 1¼ in/
30 mm wide (join where
necessary), cut to size (top and
bottom pieces to extend over
side pieces).

SECOND BORDER: 4 strips
navy print approx. 2½ in/
65 mm wide (join where
necessary), cut to size (top and
bottom pieces to extend over
side pieces).

LIGHT-COLOURED
SQUARES: 14 no. 1 RIT
squares in light print.

BINDING: Dark red print
strips 3 in/75 mm wide. Join
and prepare as on page 126.

MAKING THE QUILT

1 Cut 4 pieces of material 17 x 13 in/43 x 33 cm, 1 from red, 1
from navy, 2 from light prints. Pair a red with a light print and
a navy with a light print, right sides together. On light sides, draw
grid using no.3 template (see page 124). Draw diagonal lines both
ways exactly through corners and sew exactly ¼ in/6 mm either side
of one set of lines.

2 Cut each
square into 4
pieces. Open each
piece to form a
triangle and press
seam towards
darker colour.
Arrange pieces into
piles of mirror
images.

3 Sew each piece
from navy pile
to its mate from red
pile, matching
seams carefully.
Sew all pieces
together in a long
string to save time
and to keep them all
together.

4 *Press pieces carefully. Cut 14 squares of light material and 6 of red using no. 1 template (see page 124). Lay out the 4 remaining prints (1 red, 1 navy, 2 light) as in step 1. Follow steps 1–6 for the Amish Cot Quilt on pages 36–7 to make 48 no. 2 RIT squares, with light and dark halves.*

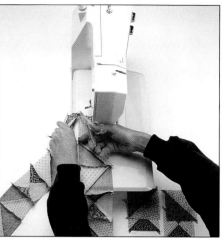

5 *Cut 6 1¾ in/45 mm squares from light print lined with Bondaweb. Appliqué to centres of red squares (see steps 2–6 on pages 42–3). Sew rows following exploded view.*

6 *Sew first rows together, taking care to align the squares.*

7 *Sew rows together. Make sure you sew them on the right way round (i.e. right sides facing) and align all seams (easy if you have been consistent in using a seam of exactly ¼ in/6 mm).*

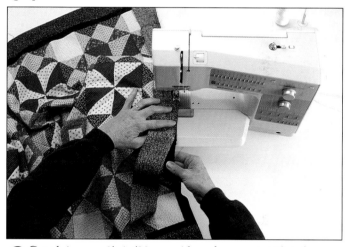

8 *Cut plain navy 1¼ in/30 mm wide and navy print 2½ in/ 65 mm wide for borders and sew on (see step 8 for Amish Cot Quilt on page 37). Press patchwork well. Cut backing fabric and wadding and sandwich all together (see page 125).*

9 *Wind bobbin to match backing and thread needle to match top (use invisible nylon thread in the needle if you prefer, so that quilting stitches do not show as you move from colour to colour). Quilt carefully along all seam lines (see page 125).*

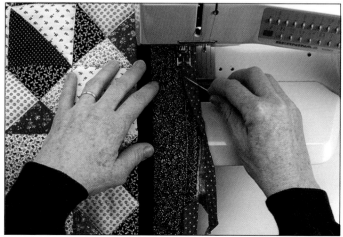

10 *Cut bias binding 3 in/75 mm wide and attach on wrong side. Fold over and stitch binding to right side, guiding it in place with a pin (see page 126).*

AMISH COT QUILT

THE AMISH COMMUNITIES of Pennsylvania (where they first settled), Ohio and Indiana are descended from the early eighteenth century Swiss Amish. They, with the Quakers and Mennonites, espoused an ascetic life in reaction to the luxurious excesses of the Catholic Church. They still live sequestered but busy lives, in, but not of, the world – the people of which are known by them as 'the English' — taking their guidance from the Bible. There is a singular beauty to Amish objects, which have the clean functional charm of Shaker accoutrements, stemming from a similar religious devotion. On visiting Lancaster County, Pennsylvania, the sense of stepping back in time is emphasized by the fact that the Amish residents do not like to own telephones, electricity, rubber tyres, contemporary farming machinery, indoor plumbing or faddish vanities like buttons, though these are now grudgingly being accepted. They do not use cars, preferring their classically elegant horse-drawn carriages and carts.

The Amish aesthetic could be well summed up by the words of Horatio Greenough, author of *The Travels, Observations, and Experiences of a Yankee Stonecutter*:

'The redundant must be pared down, the superfluous dropped, the necessary itself reduced to its simplest expression and then we shall find, whatever the organization may be, that beauty was waiting for us.'

There is more colour in an Amish interior than in Shaker homes — the walls are likely to be painted green, light blue or bright blue, and the spartan wood-furnished rooms may be enlivened by colourful glass, ceramics and textiles. Gardens, too, are filled with geometric beds brimming with bright, even garish flowers, glowing scarlet and orange against the sober white and forest green of the house walls.

Amish quilts were probably first made in the 1860s, and they have almost always been pieced using old-fashioned treadle machines. Prior to that, the women wove heavy woollen blankets as bed coverings.

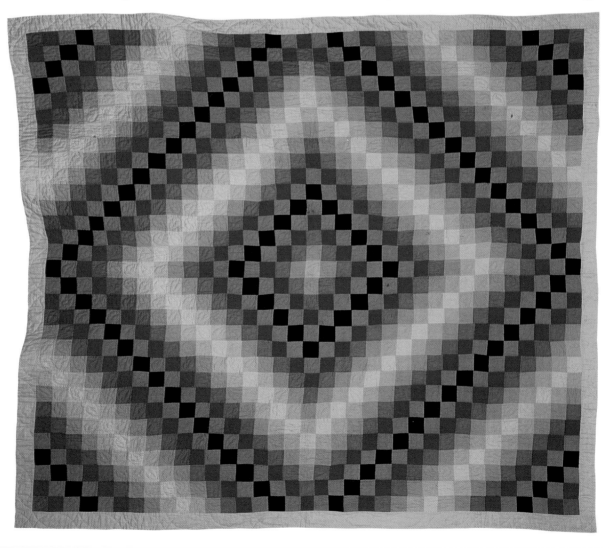

ABOVE: *A typical Amish design, simple as can be, with unexpected bright colour combinations and broad, plain borders. Quilted feathers, flowers and diamonds give textural interest.*

LEFT: *A riotous late nineteenth century 'trip around the world' quilt. Black often features in Amish and Mennonite quilt patterns, and is used to emphasize the brightness of the other colours.*

LEFT: *A Pennsylvania Mennonite quilt dating from the 1920s in a repeating rainbow stripe, with an unusual and effective bias border. Binding and backing are bright yellow calico, which shows off the fine all-over quilting.*

AMISH COT QUILT

A positive start to life, warm and bright under this variant on a simple star-burst design. Amish fabrics are plain in vibrant colours, and their quilt designs may sometimes be intricate, but they are never fussy — broadly bordered bands and rectangles of finely quilted colour are typical. Fondness for dark background and border colours gives the brighter patches an extraordinary brilliance, and gives antique Amish quilts a singularly contemporary look.

DARK EMPHATIC COLOURS have an unpredictable effect on each other — the same indigo has a green cast when placed between aquamarine and sky blue, but acquires a subtle grapey bloom when its neighbours are magenta and purple. This is part of the pleasure of working in unabashed strong colour. It forms its own relationships in a mysterious alchemy, but the total mosaic of colour is always greater than the sum of its parts.

The whole spectrum was much exploited by the canny and sophisticated Amish. Their lives may have been based on simplicity and plainness, but their sense of colour and design, of pleasing harmony and startling contrast, began a hundred years before its time.

The traditional design for a quilt consists of a central star, bar, diamond or patterned rectangle, surrounded by emphatic border strips. The elements are almost always square, triangular and rectangular. The favoured colours are red, purple, green and brilliant turquoise

against occasional browns, greys and black. Originally, Amish women dyed their own cloth using butternut, hemlock and alder bark for browns, goldenrod and black oak bark for yellows, madder for Turkey red, pokeberry for magenta and indigo for blue, and to produce greens and purples when mixed with other dyes.

The usual wadding was wool straight from the sheep, unprocessed in any way, and held in place by tiny quilting stitches, sometimes as many as twenty to the inch. Quilting designs are transferred from templates of metal, card or wood, traced in pencil, tailor's chalk, graven round with the point of a pin, or dipped in starch which dries to leave the outline of the design and can be brushed off when finished. The backing is often patterned or checked, but does not infringe the strict precepts of the Ordnung (rules of conduct) because in normal use it is invisible. At a popular and sociable quilting bee, as many as six quilts might be completed in a single day.

SHOPPING LIST

Plain cotton 45 in/115 cm wide:

Aquamarine ¼ yd/25 cm

Garnet ¼ yd/25 cm

Indigo ½ yd/45 cm

Magenta ½ yd/45 cm

Plum ½ yd/45 cm

Royal blue 1½ yd/1 m 40 cm

Scarlet 1 yd/90 cm

Shocking pink ¼ yd/25 cm

Violet ½ yd/45 cm

Plain cotton (backing) 45 in/ 115 cm wide: 1¼ yd/1 m 15 cm

Cotton bump (curtain interlining) 45 in/115 cm wide: 1¼ yd/ 1 m 15 cm

Cotton thread to match each colour

THE PALETTE
Plain shocking pink, violet, scarlet, indigo, magenta, aquamarine, plum, royal blue and garnet.

THE COMPONENTS

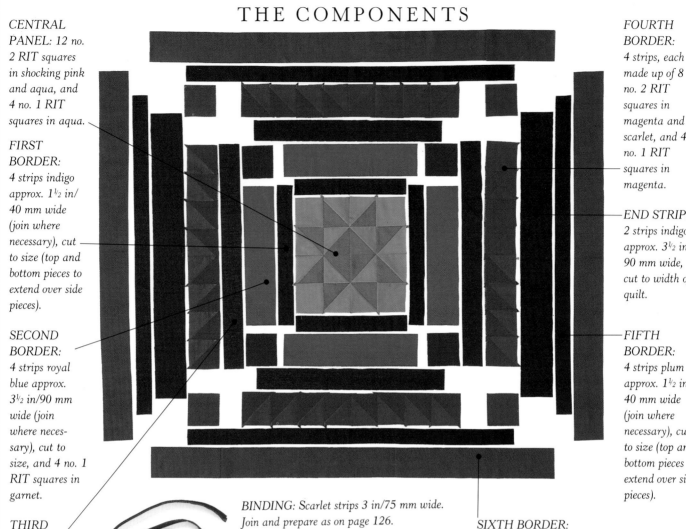

CENTRAL PANEL: 12 no. 2 RIT squares in shocking pink and aqua, and 4 no. 1 RIT squares in aqua.

FIRST BORDER: 4 strips indigo approx. 1¹⁄₂ in/ 40 mm wide (join where necessary), cut to size (top and bottom pieces to extend over side pieces).

SECOND BORDER: 4 strips royal blue approx. 3¹⁄₂ in/90 mm wide (join where neces- sary), cut to size, and 4 no. 1 RIT squares in garnet.

THIRD BORDER: 4 strips plum approx. 2¹⁄₂ in/ 65 mm wide (join where necessary), cut to size (top and bottom pieces to extend over side pieces).

FOURTH BORDER: 4 strips, each made up of 8 no. 2 RIT squares in magenta and scarlet, and 4 no. 1 RIT squares in magenta.

END STRIPS: 2 strips indigo approx. 3¹⁄₂ in/ 90 mm wide, cut to width of quilt.

FIFTH BORDER: 4 strips plum approx. 1¹⁄₂ in/ 40 mm wide (join where necessary), cut to size (top and bottom pieces to extend over side pieces).

SIXTH BORDER: 4 strips violet approx. 3¹⁄₂ in/90 mm wide (join where necessary), cut to size (top and bottom pieces to extend over side pieces).

BINDING: Scarlet strips 3 in/75 mm wide. Join and prepare as on page 126.

Use RIT square templates on page 124.

Finished quilt measures approx. 37 × 42 in/ 94 × 107 cm.

MAKING THE QUILT

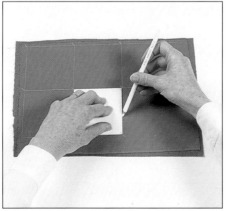

1 Using a no. 2 RIT square template (see page 124), draw a grid pattern of 6 squares on aquamarine and shocking pink, right sides facing. The template includes seam allowances, so there is no need to leave any space between the squares.

2 Using a quilter's rule, carefully mark diagonals in one direction. Only top layer of fabric needs to be marked.

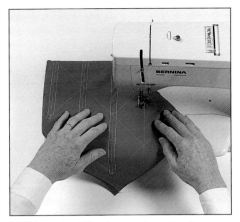

3 *Sew carefully along either side of diagonals exactly ¼ in/6 mm away in thread to match darker fabric.*

4 *There is no need to cut threads at end of each line. Sew up one side, release the needle and pull the thread into a loop. Swing the material round 180° and sew along other side of diagonal.*

5 *Trim outer edges of block of squares, then cut with scissors or an Olfa cutter along lines to produce 6 squares.*

6 *Carefully cut along central diagonal line of each of the 6 squares between stitching. Open patches to make 12 two-coloured squares.*

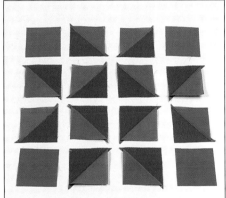

7 *Press each pink and aquamarine square firmly on the back with seam towards aqua. Lay them out and sew together as shown. Sew first into rows, then sew rows together to form centre design. Press.*

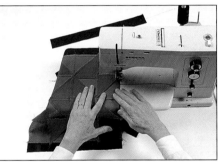

8 *Attach borders (stitch on patchwork side so needle passes exactly through point of triangle). Cut 2 strips to length of square and sew to opposite sides. Cut 2 strips to length of resulting rectangle and attach. Facing borders should always be exactly the same length. If quilt is slightly uneven, stretch or ease the quilt as you sew.*

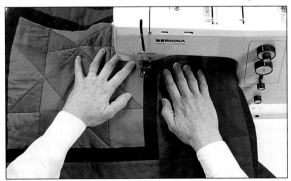

9 *Continue assembling quilt according to exploded view. When top is complete, press well with seams towards darker colours. Cut backing fabric and cotton bump slightly larger than patchwork and hold in place with sticky wadding method (see page 125). Wind bobbin to match backing and thread needle to match colour you are working on. Stitch along seam lines (see page 125).*

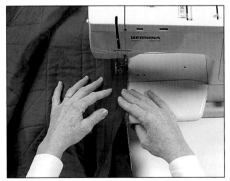

10 *Zig-zag around all edges. Cut scarlet binding 3 in/75 mm wide and attach all round quilt on wrong side (see page 126).*

11 *Fold over and stitch binding to right side with fine zig-zag stitches, guiding it in place with a pin.*

ASIAN IKAT QUILT

IKAT COMES FROM a Malay word meaning to bind or tie. The pattern is found all over the world: in Chile and Guatemala, in Europe and the Balearic Islands, the Middle East and Africa. The oldest pieces are Japanese and date from the eleventh century; there are paintings of garments resplendent with the cloudy design from ancient India.

The pattern is so universal because it is a very simple way of making richly coloured and strongly patterned fabrics without having recourse to the technology and finesse of the dyes and mordants required for block printing. Ikat gets its mysterious blurred pattern from the pre-dyeing of the warp and weft fibres before they are woven, using resist techniques. The uncontrollable nature of the method elicits the indistinct cloud and flame shapes in the finished cloth.

The ikat that interests us here is that of Central Asia, used as clothing, coverlets and tent hangings. Dyeing and weaving has always been a highly specialized and valued art among these people, and the capital of the dye world was Bokhara. Here skeins of silk and cotton were dipped in concoctions of indigo and saffron, lac, larkspur, pomegranate rind and mulberry fungus, gall nut and pistachio hulls. Dyeing and overdyeing produced a rainbow of colours culminating in the fabulous seven-colour ikat known as 'aftrang'.

The most familiar patterns are those of Turkoman carpets and Uzbek kilims, subtly transmuted from embroidery and tufted and flatweave wool to the finer fibres of silk and cotton. The design repertoire is of abstract and barely recognizable flowers and fruit, softened and blurred geometric motifs, animals, birds and insects.

With the pressures of the twentieth century, intricate motifs have been simplified. But such is the strength of tradition and the legacy of millennia of refinement, that even a childishly basic design of blocks of ruby, cerise and magenta becomes an object lesson in sumptuous painterly dazzle. In the ceremonial garments and the pieced hangings, there is extraordinary sophistication in the partnership of ikat with imported floral prints and magnificent contrasting or toning linings.

LEFT: *A vibrant interplay of printed cotton and ikat-patterned silk, embellished with braid and tassels, in a boy's 'chapan', or padded coat, dating from about 1900. A perfect demonstration of the way that ikat blends and harmonizes with contrasting colours and types of fabric.*

ABOVE: *The strong geometry of the squares and borders and the common denominator of warm cerise disciplines this glorious motley of colour and pattern into a cohesive whole. This rug, an example of nomadic patchwork known as a 'korak', was made in the mid-nineteenth century from scraps of materials made at an earlier time.*

LEFT: *A ceremonial wrapping cloth featuring the auspicious pentagram, which may have been used to cover a mirror in defence against the evil eye.*

RIGHT: *A richly complex hanging combining stripes, ikat patterns and imported printed cloth in a strongly co-ordinated colour scheme. As in the wrapping cloth, the central squares are beautifully bordered with tiny 'sawtooth' and 'flying geese' designs.*

ASIAN IKAT QUILT

A mixture of unexpected colours and unrelated patterns, patched and appliquéd in vibrant harmony, this is a quilt designed in the idiom of the nomadic tent hangings intended as a welcome to strangers and a deterrent to the evil eye. The dominant reds give unity to the scheme and are flattered by contrast with elements of black, white and orange.

CENTRAL ASIAN TEXTILES are remarkable not only for the multi-coloured richness of their silks and cottons, but also for the consummate skill with which the raw materials are put together in exuberant harmony, taking totally disparate elements and creating an unexpectedly happy marriage. Centuries-old traditional ikat designs are bordered with glowing slivers of blowsy magenta and green rose-printed cotton from Russia, and edged with a crunchy, crudely woven braid or ragged fringe. Clothing gets a glorious buzz from combining huge extrovert fuzzy geometry outside with a prim printed paisley lining or a crisp stripe in closely related but not necessarily matching colours.

Pieced squares are often used as wrapping cloths to cover such things as mirrors in superstitious deference to the evil eye. Even the geometry has significance, and when the cloths are folded in place bears a strong resemblance to the protective magic squares of the Persians. The men's straight quilted coats were worn at ceremonials and festivities and given as wedding presents to the groom. The generously cut flowing coats of the women were worn over full trousers, tapering to a narrow ankle band. Again, the best were worn to give gravitas to weddings and funerals.

Top and lining were joined together over a thin interlining with straightforward basting stitches which gave a crisp finish and ensured the coat hung in dignified folds. To add to the general air of magnificence, these regal garments were often worn in several layers in stunning tribute to the painterly eye of their creators, a testimonial to the uncanny reluctance of their glowing cumuli of colour to quarrel. They always seem to work together, making nothing so banal as mere clothes – these are works of art.

SHOPPING LIST

Cotton ikat material 45 in/
115 cm wide:
4 patterns (squares)
½ yd/45 cm each

Orange check (strips around
squares) 1 yd/90 cm

Black arrow-pattern (border)
⅔ yd/60 cm

Coarse-weave cotton 45 in/115 cm
wide:
Red (border and red squares)
1½ yd/1 m 40 cm

Black (black squares) ⅔ yd/60 cm

Natural/white (diamonds)
½ yd/45 cm

Bondaweb: 24 in/60 cm

Cotton fabric (backing) 60 in/
150 cm wide: 2 yd/1 m 80 cm

Cotton thread to match white

THE PALETTE

*Four ikat prints and one check in toning reds and oranges,
one black-patterned ikat print, and plain natural
or white, red and black.*

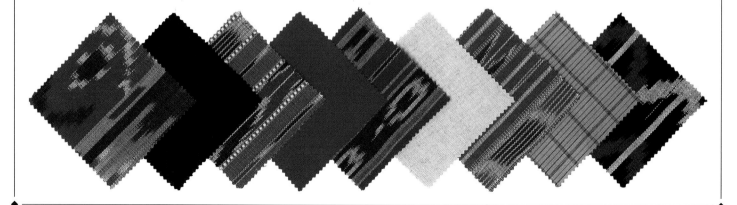

THE COMPONENTS

Finished quilt measures approx.
47 × 60 in/119 × 152 cm.

APPLIQUÉ SQUARES:
60 3½ in/90 mm black
squares, each with a small
white diamond appliquéd to
centre, and 48 3½ in/
90 mm red squares.

IKAT SQUARES:
20 8 in/20.5 cm squares in
assorted patterns, edged with
orange strips 1¼ in/
35 mm wide, and cut to fit
along edges.

FIRST BORDER: *6 strips*
black-patterned ikat approx.
2½ in/65 mm wide (join
where necessary), cut to size
(top and bottom pieces to
extend over side pieces).

SECOND BORDER:
6 strips red-patterned ikat
approx. 3 in/75 mm wide
(join where necessary), cut to
size (top and bottom pieces to
extend over side pieces).

MAKING THE QUILT

1 *Cut 60 black and 48 red 3½ in/90 mm squares.*

2 *Cut a piece of natural/white 23 × 18 in/58.5 × 46 cm, and a piece of Bondaweb 23 in/58.5 cm long. Bond to fabric.*

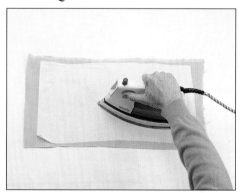

3 *Before removing Bondaweb paper, cut into 2½ in/ 65 mm squares to make 63 squares (7 rows of 9).*

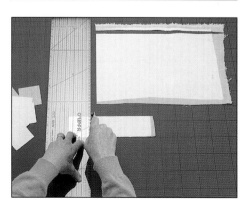

4 *Cut off small corner of each natural/white square. Iron lightly to activate adhesive, remove paper, and fold in raw edges while still sticky.*

5 Bond each natural/white square, turned through 45° to form a diamond, on to a black square.

6 Zig-zag carefully around natural/white piece to attach to black. Thread the needle with matching thread and sew carefully so that no stitches show on black.

7 Sew red and black squares together to form large squares measuring 9½ in/24 cm.

8 Cut 20 8 in/20.5 cm squares from ikat material. Cut orange check strips 1¼ in/35 mm wide and sew to ikat squares with ¼ in/6 mm seams.

9 Place all squares on floor following exploded diagram. Cut corner and side squares as shown, not corner to corner but ½ in/13 mm above. Sew squares into rows.

10 Sew rows together, taking care to align seams.

11 Cut strips of black arrow-patterned ikat 2½ in/65 mm wide, depending on pattern repeat, and of plain red 3 in/75 mm wide for borders.

12 Sew on borders (see step 8 for Amish Cot Quilt on page 37), matching seam line with exact corners of ikat squares. Press well.

13 Cut back same size as front. Sew right sides together, leaving opening large enough to turn quilt right sides out. Sew opening by hand and press.

AUSTRALIAN TAILOR'S QUILT

THE INDIGENOUS QUILTS of Australia were originally the warm and handsome fur rugs made by the Aboriginals from kangaroo or platypus skin sewn together with the sinews of the animal in question. The pioneers in the cooler south were very glad of their warmth, and they gradually evolved into more attractive objects with graded colours, decorative borders of fluffy animal tails and baize linings.

Another purely Australian quilt is the all-purpose 'wagga', named after the southern New South Wales town of Wagga Wagga where the Murrumbidgee Milling Company manufactured flour sold in jute or cotton bags. For necessary periods of sleeping out under the stars — when engaged in such pursuits as cutting back the scrub, fencing and hunting — the men were grateful for the shelter from wind and rain afforded by quilts roughly stitched from these bags. They weighed a ton, and were never really prized for their beauty: the filling of old socks, blanket scraps, worn overcoats and shredded paper militated against a smoothly elegant finished product. Large 'kangaroo' tacking stitches held the whole unwieldy bundle together.

The import of patchwork quilts first began with the philanthropic work of Elizabeth Fry in 1816. She was horrified by the degradation and lassitude among the female prisoners at Newgate, and instituted a successful campaign to allow them the dignity of work and small earnings by introducing patchwork which they could sell on arrival in Australia, if transportation was to be their fate. Few remain — perhaps people did not care to preserve quilts with a prison pedigree.

Until the twentieth century, British quilt designs predominated. There followed an exuberant outburst of highly decorated crazy quilts which gave opportunities to show off luscious fabrics and fancy stitching, and tended to be embellished with embroidered emus and wattle alongside the more usual peacock feathers and Japanese fans. They may have originally been a reaction to the Japanese exhibition in America where a rather more refined version of crazy patchwork was displayed.

From 1902, when Australia became a federal nation, there was a flowering of patriotic quilts with emblems of appliquéd emus and kangaroos adorning their patchwork tops. These were refined by the 1930s under the influence of Elizabeth George, a journalist on the *Adelaide Chronicle*, into a national passion for quilts in fashionable cream and green, celebrating the indigenous flora and fauna of the country.

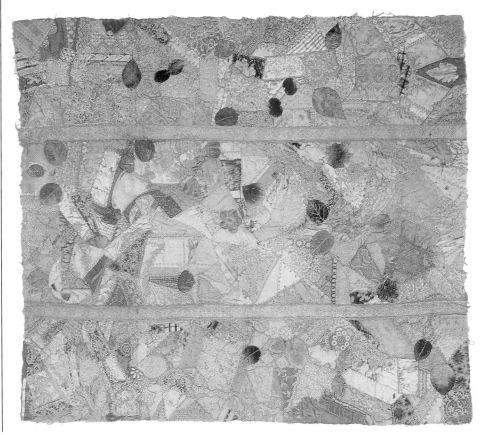

ABOVE RIGHT: *A very early Australian quilt made from cotton scraps by the Aboriginal children of Western Australia around 1840. It was worked under the guidance of Elizabeth Irwin, a benevolent Sunday school teacher with a conviction that sewing and civilization were closely allied.*

LEFT: *Australians took to crazy quilts with a passion, and this 1910 Melbourne quilt is unique in its soft autumnal colouring. The leaf motifs appear to have been hand-dyed.*

FAR RIGHT: *A lively medallion quilt made at the turn of the century, proudly centred on the kangaroo and the emu, both instantly recognizable symbols of Australia. Muted cotton prints and shirting fabrics are brought to life by invigorating dashes of red. The slightly haphazard border may be a later addition.*

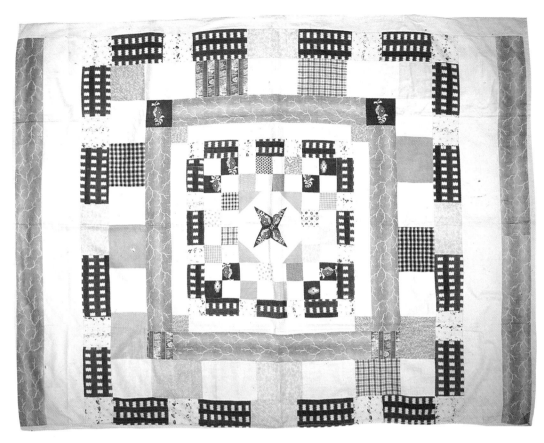

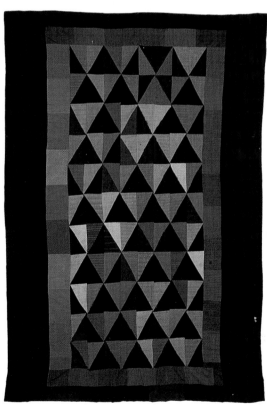

ABOVE: *Suiting samples in navy, beige, grey and pink recycled in a handsome pyramid quilt made during the dark days of the depression. Its three layers are held together with knots.*

AUSTRALIAN TAILOR'S QUILT

A natural for speedy machine stitching and a great example of making much with little. Crisp striped suiting in summery cream and sombre navy, brought to life by bands of sizzling scarlet, with the layers held together by fuzzy tassels of knotted wool, result in a quilt that embodies the best and most defiant spirit of make-do and mend.

WITH THEIR BACKS against the wall during two world wars and a depression, Australians reacted with a storm of indomitable ingenuity. The salutary principle of make-do and mend placed a value on things not usually treasured, and tailors' suiting samples became the raw materials for basic but none the less handsome quilts. Humble though they may be, slandered occasionally by the chilling pejorative 'dead men's pants', they nevertheless have sterling qualities — the weight of the wool makes them hang beautifully and imparts a comforting warmth. Simple dramatic designs of triangles and log cabin variants submit very happily to the sewing machine and speedy knotting.

It is a pity that such things became inevitably tainted by the poverty of their beginnings. They have unpretentious good looks, they are perfectly at home in a contemporary setting, and they can be constructed with a speed that must satisfy the busiest stitcher. They tended not to be quilted, but were attached to their blanket interlining and backing of cotton twill, brushed cotton or flour bag with sporadic rosettes of lazy daisy stitch or knots. They suited the casual rugged style of life in the Antipodes where they served as all-purpose throws and comforters, not requiring delicate treatment, and were the perfect covering for a night under the stars while on hunting expeditions.

A quilt does not need to be made of precious fabrics to be a minor work of art, and this no-nonsense unfussy creation bears a striking resemblance to the paintings of Paul Klee.

SHOPPING LIST

Tailor's samples or 100% wool suiting in a tight but lightweight weave 60 in/150 cm wide:

7 different pinstriped navy blues
¼ yd/25 cm each

5 different white-based checks and stripes ¼ yd/25 cm each

5 different beige tones ¼ yd/ 25 cm each

Red wool (border and binding) 60 in/150 cm wide: ¾ yd/70 cm

Plain navy wool (border) 60 in/ 150 cm wide: ¾ yd/70 cm

Plain calico (backing) 60 in/150 cm wide: 2 yd/1 m 80 cm

2oz wadding 60 in/150 cm wide: 2 yd/1 m 80 cm

Red 4-ply knitting wool (tying): 2 oz/50 g

THE PALETTE

Seven pinstriped navy blues, five white-based checks and stripes, five beige tones, and plain red and navy

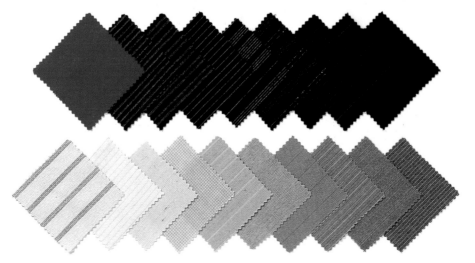

THE COMPONENTS

*Finished quilt measures approx.
51 × 57 in/130 × 145 cm.*

Use template on page 124.

TRIANGLES: *Made
from 28 dark- and 28
light-coloured rectangles.*

FIRST BORDER:
*4 strips red approx.
2 in/50 mm wide (join
where necessary), cut to
size (top and bottom
pieces to extend over side
pieces).*

BINDING: *Red strips
3 in/75 mm wide. Join and
prepare as on page 126.*

SECOND BORDER:
*4 strips assorted beige
tones approx. 5 in/13 cm
wide (join where
necessary), cut to size
(top and bottom pieces to
extend over side pieces).*

THIRD BORDER:
*4 strips navy approx.
4 in/10 cm wide (join
where necessary), cut to
size (top and bottom
pieces to extend over side
pieces).*

MAKING THE QUILT

1 *Use template on page 124
to cut 28 light and 28 dark
rectangles. The triangles of this
quilt are pieced in random
order so choose an assortment
of fabrics.*

2 *Divide the light rectangles
into 2 piles of 14. Take one
pile, and draw a line from top
left to lower right exactly from
corner to corner. On remaining
rectangles draw line from top
right to bottom left.*

3 *Place each light rectangle
right sides together with a
dark one, one piece turned
through 45° so that they align
asymmetrically along the
diagonal on the light piece. Pin
to secure.*

4 *Stitch exactly ¼ in/6 mm
either side of diagonal lines.
Remove pins and cut in two
along drawn lines.*

5 *Press seams open. Make 2 piles of rectangles, each the mirror-image of the other, so that they will form light and dark pyramids when paired.*

6 *Arrange pieces at random according to exploded diagram. Sew together with ¼ in/6 mm seams to form rows.*

7 *When sewing pieces together be very careful to match seam lines. Press seams so that they lie open.*

8 *Sew rows together. Use larger seam allowance of ½ in/13 mm. The seam must be a line from the exact point of one pyramid to the next. Press.*

9 *Cut a quantity of 5 in/13 cm wide strips of different tones of beige. Cut strips into varying lengths from 2 in/5 cm to 8 in/20.5 cm.*

10 *Join the lengths at random to form borders long enough to go all round quilt. Press well.*

11 *For borders, cut strips of red 3 in/ 75 mm wide, and navy 4 in/10 cm wide and sew on with beige strips (see step 8 for Amish Cot Quilt on page 37). Press well.*

12 *Attach backing and 2 oz wadding (see page 125). Zig-zag around edge and trim excess. Cut binding 3 in/75 mm wide and attach (see page 126).*

13 *Thread large-eyed needle with 4-ply red wool and tie quilt at the point of each pyramid with double knot. Cut ends to ¾ in/20 mm and tease out.*

BRITISH SOLDIER'S QUILT

AKING QUILTS WAS not the sole monopoly of women — some quite extraordinary examples have been created by men, notably tailors, soldiers and sailors. The latter two presumably because they had time on their hands when confined on long journeys or in hospital, and the former because the raw materials were abundantly available.

Soldiers' quilts are remarkable for the neatness and precision of their designs and the brilliant kaleidoscopic richness of the vast number of tiny patches used in their construction. Until khaki became the military norm, soldiers were proudly visible on the field of battle in an array of bright primary colours with plenty of lively red usually set off by blue, black, brown, yellow, olive and cream.

Few sailors' quilts survive, and the best known was executed by Nicholas White while he was working on the whaling ship *Balaena* in the late nineteenth century. It is an astonishing kaleidoscope of Turkey red and white cotton pieces taken from sample books. They radiate from a central medallion, and while the quilt does not have the disciplined regularity of a soldier's work, it is charged with energetic intricacy. James Cox, a sailor serving in HMS *Victory* in 1865, made a quilt with a more regular and masculine air from diamonds of red, black and white felt embroidered with flags.

In general, tailors' quilts tend to be sombre and utilitarian, although Walter Scott, a Northumbrian master tailor, made a dazzling virtuoso quilt of cloud-shaped appliquéd patches of blue suiting in the late nineteenth century as magnificent self-advertisement.

For wildly extrovert exception to sobriety there is a trio of pictorial designs that appear to owe more to the cartoon-like motifs of African Fante flags than to staid British tailoring. These depict biblical scenes and marvels of engineering in a quilt by James Williams, a tailor of Wrexham, made in the ten years between 1842 and 1852; ships and scenery and wise saws in 'The Royal Clothograph' which took John Monro, a tailor from Paisley, eighteen years to complete; and ships, royal emblems and chivalric figures stitched over a period of 1,650 hours by David Robertson of Falkirk and finished in 1853.

All of these quilts, except Nicholas White's, have something noticeably masculine about them. But two characters, famous in their part of the world, concocted marvels of lady-like delicacy. George Gardiner worked in the picturesquely named Dirt Pot, Allenheads, towards the end of the nineteenth century and was famous for his fine quilting on wholecloth; and Joe the Quilter of Hexham, who was born in 1745, made exceedingly pretty chintz quilts.

LEFT: *More than 5,500 1-inch squares in glowing colours contribute to the stained-glass brilliance of this nineteenth century soldier's quilt from Northern Ireland. It measures 58×78 in/ 147.5×198 cm and was once backed with blue wool, now reduced to tatters, a victim of fond usage.*

RIGHT: *A mosaic of tiny squares of bright wool in the regimental colours of the Indian Army. Once surrounded by a fringe, the quilt still retains a fine border.*

ABOVE: *A late nineteenth century stable boy's quilt in earthy tweeds and woollens, possibly horse blankets. The 'variable star' design is held to the plain wool backing by regular diamond quilting.*

LEFT: *Nicholas White's renowned* Balaena *quilt, made while he was steward of this ship and the* Terra Nova *in the late nineteenth century.*

BRITISH SOLDIER'S QUILT

Few but the most fanatical have the time to stitch 15,000 tiny squares of wool, but the strong colours and the clean geometry of military quilts can easily be translated to suit the twentieth century pace of life. The result has proper regimental precision in a bold crop of military colours. The wool twill top and army blanket lining are weighty enough to require no interlining.

SOLDIERS AND SAILORS have always had to be self-reliant, and many have turned to the traditionally feminine arts of needlework and knitting to while away long and unrelieved hours of boredom. Wounded soldiers confined to a hospital bed occasionally made positive use of their time to piece together thousands of tiny squares cut from the heavy woollen fabric of uniforms. In World War Two, patchwork pieces were still being sent to prisoners of war.

Until universal khaki was introduced after the Boer war, soldiers were resplendent in a dazzling palette of red, blue, gold, black, green and pink, and up to fifteen colours of uniform were sometimes represented in soldiers' quilts, most of which were made in the years between 1869 and 1900. Curiously, although the woollen fabrics were often heavy and difficult to work, this seemed to act as a challenge to the skill of the worker — a surprising number are constructed of tiny pieces barely one centimetre square. It is

not unusual for a soldier's quilt to contain over 5,000 pieces, and competitive zeal drove some men to the unimaginable feat of sewing together 12,887 and even 15,500 confetti-sized scraps of wool in just one quilt. The result was too heavy to require filling, and too stiff to need quilting. They were often finished with a straightforward cotton backing and a fringe around the edge.

The designs were always strongly geometric and the pieces usually square. Occasionally this rich mosaic of colour was not enough for its creator, who might further embellish his work with a motif or two picked out in beads.

The designs are almost always based on small square patches worked in concentric blocks of colour and then surrounded by a heavy border. The squares tend to be worked end-on as diamonds, and the tiny stitching may be the work of several hands under the guidance of one mind. Very rarely is there any fault in the working out or assembly of the design.

SHOPPING LIST

Closely woven wool, light coat or
heavy suit weight:
78 red squares ½ yd/45 cm
38 dark yellow squares ½ yd/45 cm
43 off-white squares ½ yd/45 cm
52 teal blue squares ½ yd/45 cm
44 khaki squares ½ yd/45 cm
102 black squares 1 yd/90 cm
(Total: 357 squares)

THE PALETTE
*Plain black, red, teal blue,
off-white, khaki and dark yellow*

THE COMPONENTS

Finished quilt measures approx. 37 × 44 in/ 94 × 112 cm.

PATTERN BLOCKS: 357 2½ in/65 mm squares in 6 different colours, sewn into strips then blocks for easier assembly.

BORDER: 4 strips black approx. 2 in/50 mm wide, cut to size (top and bottom pieces to extend over side pieces).

BINDING: Black strips 3 in/75 mm wide. Join and prepare as on page 126.

MAKING THE QUILT

1 Cut enough strips of each colour 2½ in/65 mm wide.

2 Cut strips into 2½ in/65 mm squares and stack according to colour.

3 Lay out the pieces according to the exploded diagram. This detail shows the formation of the block on the far right of the second row. Repeat for all blocks.

4 *Assemble each block row by row using ¹/₄ in/6 mm seams. (This measurement is critical — if you are not accurate in your seaming the squares will not align.)*

5 *Press seams in each row in opposite directions to lessen bulk when rows are sewn together.*

6 *Sew rows together to make blocks, taking care to align all seams.*

7 *Steam press front and back carefully and heavily to reduce bulk. Working on reverse side first, press all seams in same direction, then turn over and press right side so that the surface is flat and the seams do not show through as ridges.*

8 *Following exploded diagram, sew blocks together to form 4 rows of 3 blocks each.*

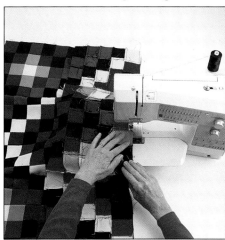

9 *Sew rows together. Press well, clipping seams where necessary. Cut black border strips 2 in/50 mm wide and attach (see step 8 for Amish Cot Quilt on page 37).*

10 *Cut backing blanket to same size as finished top and catch together with large zig-zag stitches.*

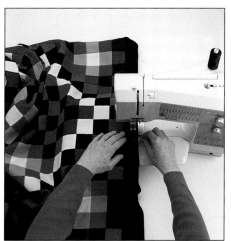

11 *Cut binding 3 in/75 mm wide. Fold, press and attach (see page 126). This quilt is heavy enough to need no interlining, quilting or tying.*

BRITISH STRIPPY QUILT

THE NORTH COUNTRY strippy quilt is typically executed in broad bold stripes of Turkey red and white cotton. The first recorded example of this style dates from the end of the eighteenth century and is made from much-patched and mended chintz, cotton and calico. Another early version dates from 1840 and comes from the Isle of Man, where there was a strong tradition of quilts in sonorous, almost Amish colours of crimson black, dark blue and green.

Strippy quilts are most common in the north of England and Wales — Northumberland and County Durham particularly took the dramatic and simple design to their hearts and produced thousands between 1860 and 1930. The English versions tend to be brighter than the Welsh, whose makers favoured a sombre palette of funereal purple, magenta and black, the quilts often being made of wool. North country strippies use colours in startling contrasts — cerulean, mustard, scarlet, all with white or patterned fabrics in conjunction with plain.

Pastels feature too — pink, blue, cream and mauve in various combinations.

The basic stripes can be enlivened in a number of ways by adding sawtooth edges, making pieced zig-zags or patched diamonds.

The quilting was usually done in a border design working along each strip one at a time. This had the advantage of being easier to design and organize in a frame than medallion and wholecloth quilts, in which the pattern of the entire top had to be borne in mind all the time. Thus strippies tend to have feathers, plaits, tulips and zig-zags stitched along their slices of colour.

The strippy was often dual purpose, being stripped on one side and wholecloth on the other, so that the fashion-conscious invalid could turn the quilt to the more prestigious plain side on the arrival of a doctor or visiting dignitary. It was always the quilting rather than the piecing which was intended to impress and over which great care was taken.

LEFT: *The ever-popular partnership of Turkey red and white cotton in a wedding quilt from West Cornforth, County Durham, made in 1870. Its maker set herself an unusual problem by ignoring the confines of the strips in her quilting design, thereby creating a wholecloth pattern on the other side, resplendent with a central true lovers' knot and feather pattern borders.*

BELOW: *Wave-quilted pink and patterned cotton, the tiny print adding a texture of its own in contrast to the stitching.*

ABOVE: *An early twentieth century quilt with wide strips of blue and white cotton quilted in the usual manner along the strips, the blue featuring a rose in concentric rings and the white a simple plait design.*

LEFT: *A simple 1930s strippy quilt from County Durham in alternating bands of plain white and red and white stripes. The fine cotton interlining and plain white backing are held together with simple running-stitch chevrons. A narrow border of red and white spots contributes a graphic finish.*

BRITISH STRIPPY QUILT

The nostalgic partnership of block-printed pattern and plain eau-de-nil cotton lawn combine in a quilt that could have graced the bedroom of a 1930s mansion. The pale peppermint green stripes effectively show off a simple but attractive heraldic quilting design, all sinuous curves and curlicues. Lined in butter-yellow, it is interlined with cotton bump to give substance.

ONE OF THE great undervalued examples of British design, strippy quilts are a sublime answer to the machine age. Their popularity was probably due in part to the ease with which they could be run up by machine, and their striking simplicity has made them classics ever since. In the past, however, the quilting was the proudest attribute and this was accomplished by hand in hours of wearisome stitching. Nowadays, with more amenable fillings that do not need to be minutely locked into place, the quilting does not need to be so fine and can be whizzed together by machine.

If the complexities of our quilting pattern are beyond the grasp of you or your machine, it is perfectly acceptable, in fact traditional, to use an unadorned wave pattern meandering from the top to the bottom. An old blanket makes a good filling, as does cotton bump or, more expensively, wool domette — the heavier the interlining the better the finished quilt will hang. You can also experiment with different casing materials — strips of lightweight wool work very successfully, and linen is a traditional fabric with unique draping qualities.

You do not need to be a genius to calculate quantities or to cut and piece the strips. There are usually between nine and thirteen strips, each between 9 in/ 23 cm and 12 in/30 cm wide. Strong plain colours work well, as do combinations of plain and small all-over patterns. The edges can be plain or finished with a narrow binding. However you put it together, the indigenous British strippy is a tradition to be proud of.

SHOPPING LIST

Pre-shrunk cotton lawn
36 in/90 cm wide:

Pale green 2 yd/1 m 80 cm

Toning small all-over print
2 yd/1 m 80 cm

Butter-yellow (backing and binding) 4 yd/3 m 65 cm

4 oz Terylene wadding 60 in/
150 cm wide: 2 yd/1 m 80 cm

Cotton thread to match each colour

THE PALETTE
One floral print and plain pale green

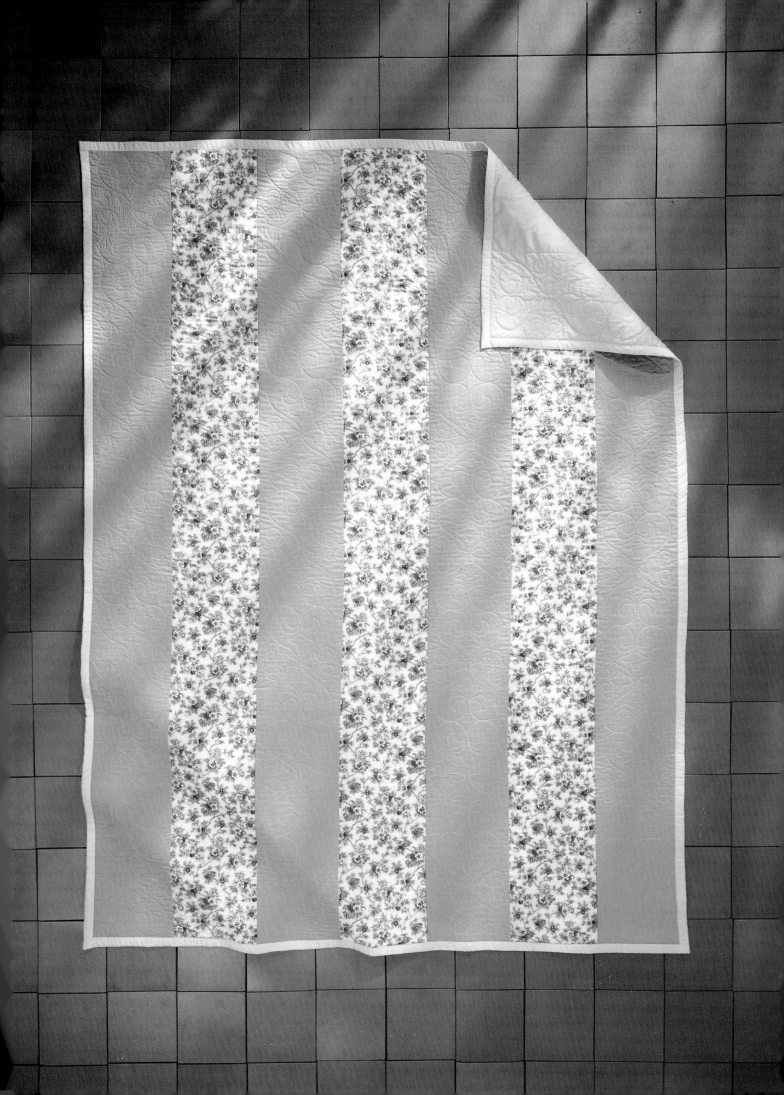

THE COMPONENTS

Finished quilt measures approx. 54 × 68 in/ 37 × 173 cm.

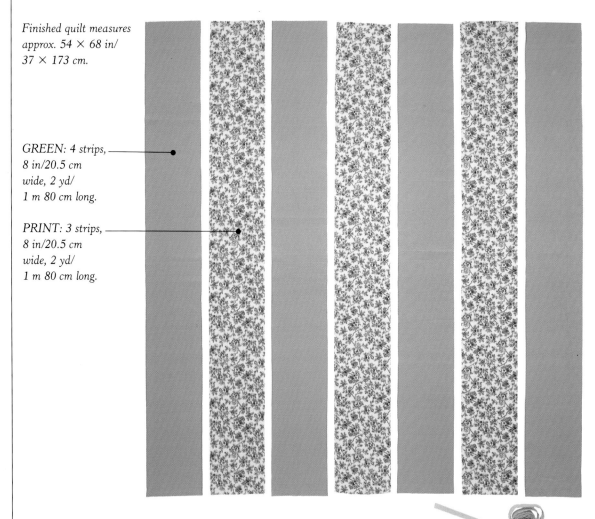

GREEN: 4 strips, 8 in/20.5 cm wide, 2 yd/ 1 m 80 cm long.

PRINT: 3 strips, 8 in/20.5 cm wide, 2 yd/ 1 m 80 cm long.

BINDING: Butter-yellow strips 3 in/75 mm wide. Join and prepare as on page 126.

MAKING THE QUILT

1 *Press fabric accurately lengthwise in 8 in/20.5 cm folds. The creases will act as a cutting guide.*

2 *Cut 3 strips 72 × 8 in/183 × 20.5 cm of floral pattern following pressed guide lines.*

3 *Cut 4 strips 72 × 8 in/183 × 20.5 cm of pale green.*

4 *Sew alternating green and floral strips together as shown in layout. Once all the pieces have been joined together, press seams towards green strips.*

5 *Spray wadding with adhesive. Attach quilt top to wadding by sticky wadding method (see page 125). Turn over and repeat with yellow quilt backing. Catch the edges of quilt top, wadding and backing together with wide zig-zag stitches and trim.*

6 *Trace quilting pattern (see page 123) on to a piece of transparent acetate. Cut stencil with sharp scalpel, leaving lots of bridges.*

7 *Transfer quilting design to plain green strips using water-erasable pen. (It is important to use the right pen as the quilt can then be sprayed or rinsed to remove any traces of ink without streaking or running.)*

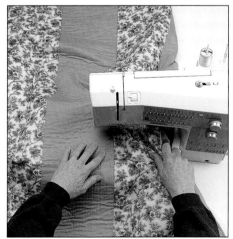

8 *Thread needle and wind bobbin to match top and backing. Stitch carefully along all seam lines on flatter (floral) side of each seam (see page 125).*

9 *Lower feed dog and replace presser foot with darning foot. Quilt on pen lines (see page 125). Attach 3 in/75 mm border of yellow strips (see page 126).*

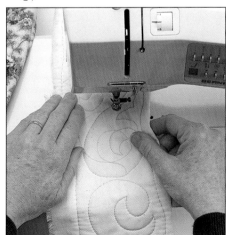

10 *Practise your quilting tension and technique on a piece of scrap material before working on the quilt itself.*

CANADIAN SHIRTING QUILT

THE INDIANS WHO inhabited Canada originally decorated their clothing with leather appliqué patterns and their ceremonial robes with good luck talismans. Furs and animal skins obviated the need for textiles, and it was furs and animal skins that first attracted foreign settlers. In the early seventeenth century, intrepid French fur traders built log cabins in what eventually became Quebec, Trois Rivières and Montreal. The women brought clothing and bedding with them, and thriftily re-used worn fabrics, dyed to uncharacteristic brightness with the natural colours introduced to them by the native Indians, and pieced together to make 'catalognes' or patched coverlets.

These pioneers were joined in time by Scottish and German settlers who brought a taste for goose-feather comforters and wholecloth linsey-woolsey (a linen-wool mix) quilts embellished with fine stitching or embroidery. The Amish and Mennonites from the Black Forest and Swiss Alps left a considerable legacy of brilliantly coloured, finely stitched plain quilts, or quilts appliquéd with hearts, distlefinks (goldfinches) and hex signs intended to ensure good fortune.

In the nineteenth century, sophisticated fabrics became much more easily available, and richly patterned chintzes were used entire and uncut in wholecloth quilts by the wealthy, or as 'broderie perse' motifs and printed medallions in pieced quilts by everyone else.

Woollen utility quilts in plain and pieced blocks of browns, blues, oranges, greys, reds and creams are still made in a tradition that goes back to the early 1800s and beyond. Unfortunately, very few antique quilts remain because of the fragility of the fabrics, which were already old and worn by the time they were transformed into bed covers, and because the quilts were then used constantly for all sorts of undignified purposes until they disintegrated completely.

LEFT: *Subtle colours of nineteenth century printed cottons in a comparatively urbane and sophisticated quilt composed of concentric rows of right-angled triangles. Completed around 1860, the quilt is a splendid achievement on the part of E. Bruels from York County, Ontario, who was eighty-seven years old at the time.*

ABOVE: *Handwoven wool in a handsome utility quilt made in Orangeville, Dufferin County, about 1865. Like the cotton quilt opposite, this was worked outwards from the centre, and the patched and hoarded scraps have been carefully chosen to make a harmonious design. The lining is thick tan cotton, the wadding wool, held in place with shell pattern quilting, and the whole is bound with black velvet.*

RIGHT: *More homespun wool, and another example of pleasant harmony resulting from a limited palette. The simple design of bordered blocks in a chequerboard pattern is surprisingly rarely seen and has great charm. Printed fabrics were expensive and hard to come by but such combinations of checks and stripes have a richness of their own.*

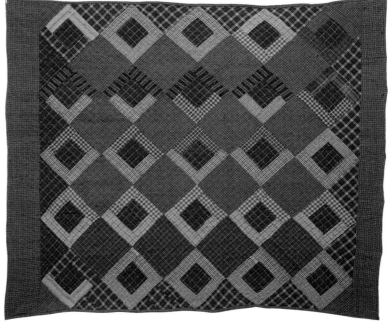

Canadian Shirting Quilt

Contemporary thrift — this no-nonsense quilt is made from cotton shirts once the collars and cuffs have frayed: today's urban equivalent to the heavy homespun worn by loggers and trappers. Fine woven checks and stripes in a very basic design have an understated elegance, and tying imparts an attractive puffiness to the finished quilt.

THE PIONEERS WHO settled in Canada came initially from Europe and Britain, and while the women brought their quilting expertise with them, the wild country they colonized had none of the raw materials with which they were familiar. 'Boughten' fabric was scarce and costly, so people tended to spin and weave their own. Wool or linen homespun was the staple textile, dyed with natural colours — butternut, goldenrod, logwood black, madder and indigo — using sour milk or slaked lime as a bleach, and 'chamber lye' (human urine) as a mordant. Indeed, shop-bought cloth was such an expensive extravagance, home weaving was almost a necessity, though women might take their own homespun yarn to professional weavers to be made into cloth. Printed fabric was a luxury that could not be achieved with the primitive equipment available, so woven checks and stripes in various permutations had to serve for pattern and adornment.

Warm clothing and bedding was essential in the freezing winter cold, and every scrap of fabric was recycled over and over again. On the coast, frayed woollen shirts were transformed into hooked rugs. In Ontario, worn workshirts became children's clothes, these became quilt-patches, and when the quilts finally fell apart, the shreds were used to block draughty window-frames and doors.

The wadding was usually carded wool or cotton; feathers and goose-down were also warm and light. As the year advanced, women stitched furiously to be ready with warm bedding by the time the snow came. As a result, Canadian utility quilts had a casual approach to design, and quilting was sometimes replaced by tying — a speedy substitute that suits contemporary wadding materials.

The predominant blue of this quilt is enlivened by elements of brown and red. Fine cotton shirting is easier to come by than heavy homespun, but checked and striped wool, brushed cotton or even outworn striped pyjamas are closer to the original and have a more rustic charm. Lightweight Terylene wadding has been used, held in place with knots of crochet cotton. Cotton bump or a woollen blanket would suit a thicker and softer fabric. The backing is slightly heavier cotton in a toning colour.

SHOPPING LIST
---

10 fine pinstriped or checked cotton lawn shirts or different tones of blue and brown checked and striped material 36 in/ 90 cm wide:

5 different light tones ½ yd/ 45 cm each

5 different darker tones ½ yd/ 45 cm each

Cotton fabric (backing): 4 yd/ 3 m 65 cm

Checked cotton fabric (binding): ¾ yd/70 cm

2 oz Terylene wadding 60 in/ 150 cm wide: 2 yd/1 m 80 cm

No. 10 crochet cotton and sharp needle for tying

THE PALETTE
Five light- and five dark-toned stripes and checks

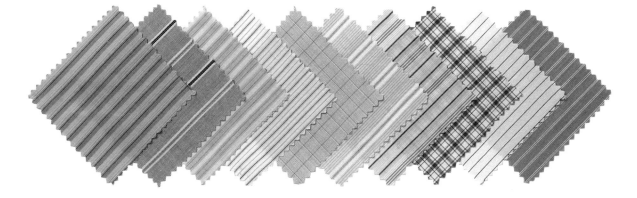

THE COMPONENTS

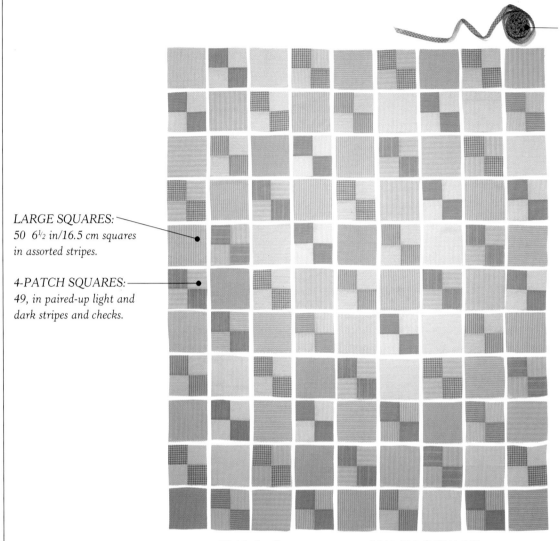

BINDING: Checked bias strips 3 in/75 mm wide. Join and prepare as on page 126.

LARGE SQUARES:
50 6½ in/16.5 cm squares
in assorted stripes.

4-PATCH SQUARES:
49, in paired-up light and
dark stripes and checks.

Finished quilt measures approx. 54 × 66 in/137 × 168 cm.

MAKING THE QUILT

1 *This is the perfect use for worn shirts, abandoned because of tattered collars and cuffs. Remove sleeves and open to make flat pieces.*

2 *Using 6½ in/16.5 cm square template, cut 50 squares. You should be able to get 5 from each sleeve, 4 from each front, and 9 from the back of each shirt.*

3 *Cut enough 3½ in/90 mm wide strips of assorted stripes and checks to make 49 4-patch squares.*

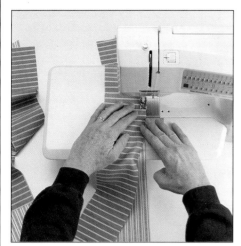

4 Sew lengthwise striped strips to crosswise striped strips in pairs. Press strips with seams towards darker side.

5 Cut strips across in 3½ in/90 mm widths to make sets of rectangles composed of 2 different square patches.

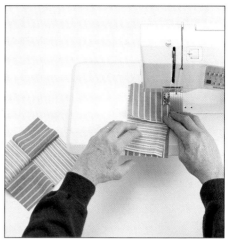

6 Turn alternate pieces upside-down, align seams and sew together to make 6 in/15 cm squares of 4 patches each. Press all squares.

7 Sew 4-patch squares alternating with plain squares to make 11 rows of 9 squares.

8 Sew rows together to form quilt top. Cut backing fabric and wadding slightly larger than patchwork and sandwich everything together with sticky wadding method (see page 125).

9 Secure along edges with wide zig-zag stitches. Trim excess fabric and wadding.

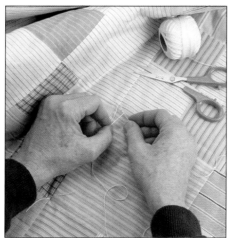

10 Using no. 10 crochet cotton, tie front to back at corners of all 6 in/15 cm squares with double knots. Trim ends to 1½ in/40 mm.

11 Fold fabric diagonally and cut 3 in/75 cm wide strips on the bias. Join together to give enough length to bind entire quilt and attach (see page 126).

FRENCH BOUTIS QUILT

INDIAN BLOCK-PRINTED cottons from the seventeenth century onwards had a massive impact on every aspect of fashionable life, from clothing to furnishing and quilts. Their subtle and ancient mastery of dye and mordant produced fast colours and intricate designs unparalleled in the West until the mid-eighteenth century when the secrets of the complex processes began to be analysed and emulated.

India was the birthplace of the delicious chintzes that never fail to marry well together, and the richly patterned palampores that graced the beds of the wealthy. Its was the genius that first created intricate all-over prints and paisley designs, and it contributed the simple and effective device of surrounding the central panel of a quilt with a broad toning border to enclose and enrich the pattern within.

Besides its beauty, Indian cloth was relatively dye-fast — a vital consideration with quilts which can never recover from fading or bleeding colours — and bales of the sumptuously patterned cotton were eagerly snapped up by the fashion-conscious needlewomen of Europe, Great Britain and America.

It all began in 1592, when a Spanish ship was captured by an English privateer, and its wonderful cargo of lawns, printed calicoes and palampores excited enough interest to lead to the establishment of the East India Company in 1600. Exactly a hundred years later, the import of chintz into England was banned, and in 1720 its use in clothing and furnishings was also prohibited. To little avail — the ban simply meant that import revenue was denied the government, and black market fabric was smuggled in to satisfy the passion for Indian textiles. Smuggling did not make for economy, and consequently 'broderie perse' evolved to make the best use of every tiny curlicue or tendril of the precious pattern. Printed cloth in America and Great Britain took decades to come anywhere near the glorious richness of Indian techniques and designs, and even then came dangerously close to straying from the path of good taste by the introduction of aniline dyes which had nothing of the harmonious alchemy that natural dyes could produce.

Palampores, with their resplendent tree of life at the centre, had a direct influence on the quilting approach of European women. In Holland, Portugal and around Marseilles, finely printed bright fabrics were given similar broad mitred borders on quilts. Luminous combinations of colour and mutually flattering motifs were characteristic of this little-documented fine art. The quilting was usually functional rather than decorative — straight lines or diamonds being the norm.

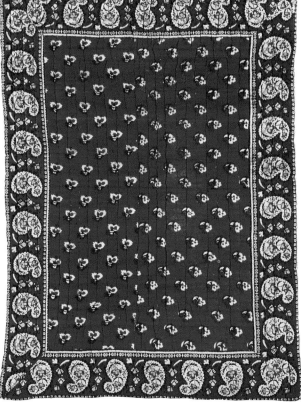

ABOVE: *A nineteenth century Indian-print quilt from Holland, pieced with a fine disregard for perfection, and all the better for it. The colours of the somewhat disjointed centre are repeated and enriched in the mitred border.*

LEFT: *The working clothes of a Provençal peasant girl in the nineteenth century. The attractive skirt is unusual, made from patched strips of cotton in toning blues and browns and quilted with simple diamonds – plain or patterned unpieced cotton with more elaborate quilting was the norm.*

FAR LEFT: *A heavily padded Dutch palampore whose swirling floral design forms the basis for the quilting pattern – its extravagant fronds and tendrils are repeated on the brilliant yellow of the backing. The border, in toning reds, is an essential element in the design.*

FRENCH BOUTIS QUILT

Provençal market cotton in complementary red and green, enclosed by a somewhat more refined mitred border and evenly quilted, results in a charming hybrid of French rusticity and Indian richness. A plain dark green cotton lining shows off the close diamond quilting, and cotton bump (curtain interlining) for wadding gives the quilt substance and weight.

THE FRENCH HAVE a tradition for simple patchwork quilts using small checks and prints pieced in strips of squares and diamonds, and medallions bordered by concentric strips of plain and pieced cloth. But where they really excel is in their boutis — Provençal quilts of block-printed cotton with strong Indian overtones, in radiant colours, bordered in wide bands of print and finely quilted. There is nothing to beat the rich mix of colour: vibrant partnerships of turmeric yellow with cinnabar and cherry red, or magenta with navy and a particularly piercing sky-blue, all sprigged and paisley-patterned and stitched with tiny diamonds. Young girls would vie with each other to produce the most glorious and intricate combinations of colour, patterns and fine quilting. Like Madame Defarge, they would use their handiwork to convey messages, though of a more romantic nature — keys and scissors, symbols of happy marriage, birds and flowers interlace around the borders of quilts and petticoats. Padded with cotton, they gave welcome protection against the vicious mistral wind.

The delicately patterned wood-block printed cottons came to be known simply as 'les indiennes', despite the fact that from the seventeenth century many came to Marseilles from Turkey and the Levant where cheaper reproductions were being printed. In 1648 the first 'atelier' was set up in Marseilles, and thirty years later, another in Avignon. Imported Indian cloth was banned in 1686, but almost a century passed before the French fabrics could emulate the colourfast brightness and subtlety of the 'indiennes'.

However, they did achieve an expertise of their own, which still flourishes in the work of one or two manufacturers. Wood-block prints are a thing of the past except for the very wealthy, but the fine traditional prints have been carefully and convincingly transferred to copper rollers to enable mass production.

Provençal cottons have an extraordinary capacity to co-ordinate well together — they are meant to be used in exuberant conjunction with each other. The all-important border designs are designed to give cohesion to contrasting colour and pattern.

SHOPPING LIST
---

2 different Provençal cotton prints with regular geometric patterns 36 in/90 cm wide:

Green print 2 yd/1 m 80 cm

Black print ¾ yd/70 cm

Red (binding) ½ yd/45 cm

Floral border: 12 yd/11 m

Plain green fabric (backing) 48 in/120 cm wide: 1¾yd/1 m 60 cm

Cotton bump (curtain interlining) 48 in/120 cm wide: 1¾ yd/1 m 60 cm

Cotton thread to match each colour

THE PALETTE

Two geometric prints and one floral border.

THE COMPONENTS

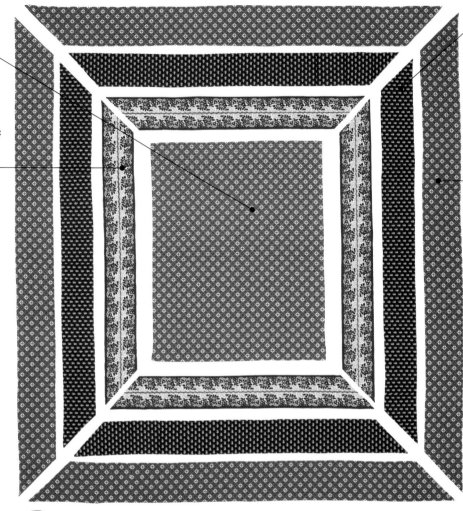

CENTRE PANEL:
24 × 30 in/61 ×
76 cm green print.

FIRST BORDER:
4 strips floral border
fabric (sewn together
lengthwise to double its
width), widths 33 in/
84 cm long, lengths
38 in/97 cm long (join
where necessary), with
ends cut across
diagonally.

SECOND BORDER:
4 strips black print
approx. 4½ in/11 cm
wide, widths 41 in/
104 cm long, lengths
47 in/119 cm long
(join where necessary),
with ends cut across
diagonally.

THIRD BORDER:
4 strips green print
approx. 5½ in/14 cm
wide, widths 52 in/
132 cm long, lengths
57 in/145 cm long
(join where necessary),
with ends cut across
diagonally.

BINDING: Red strips
3 in/75 mm wide.
Join and prepare as
on page 126.

Finished quilt measures approx. 51 × 56 in/130 × 142 cm.

MAKING THE QUILT

1 Cut green print into strips on pattern repeat about 5½ in/14 cm wide. Cut 5 or 6 depending on width and join where necessary.

2 Do the same with black print, 4½ in/11.5 cm wide. Cut green print rectangle lengthwise along pattern 24 × 30 in/60 × 76 cm.

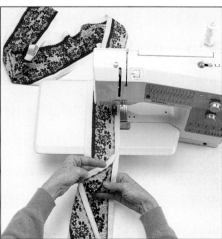

3 Sew border lengthwise to double width, matching inside seams so that the pattern repeats as a mirror image once opened out.

4 *Cut borders slightly longer than necessary to fit around rectangular panel and sew strips together according to exploded view.*

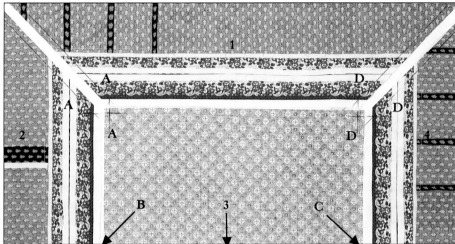

5 *To sew mitred corners, mark ⅝ in/15 mm seam allowances around central rectangle and on narrower edge of 4 borders. Mark width of rectangle on border to find exact points of corners. Use a 45° triangle to mark seamline either side of each border to point of corner.*

6 *Sew border 1 to rectangle, matching points A to D. Sew on border 2, matching points B to A. Exactly on point A, stop with needle in down position.*

7 *With needle down, make a quarter-turn by swinging work round 45°.*

8 *Continue sewing from A along diagonal, matching border patterns and seams. Repeat for borders 3 and 4. Press and attach top to backing (see page 125).*

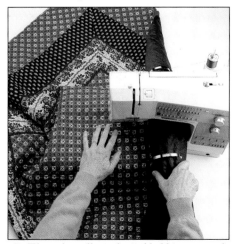

9 *Thread needle and wind bobbin to match quilt top and back. Using walking foot, quilt centre diagonally in both directions (see page 125). Hold quilt with bicycle clips.*

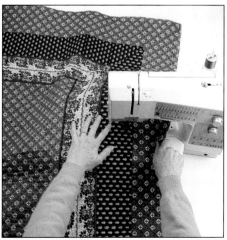

10 *Quilt borders in straight lines about 1–2 in/25–50 mm apart following printed pattern.*

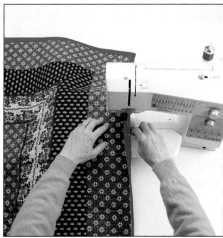

11 *Cut binding 3 in/75 mm wide and attach (see page 126).*

Hawaiian Appliqué Wall-Hanging

THE PACIFIC ISLANDS of Polynesia — Hawaii in the north, and the Cook, Society and Austral Islands in the south — all have slightly different but similar quilting traditions, of which variants on Hawaiian appliqué are the most familiar. All the islands produce appliqué and patchwork which is usually worked in squares, diamonds or hexagons. The pieced quilt style, and possibly the art of quilting itself, was introduced to the islands by missionaries from the London Missionary Society after 1827.

Polynesian patchwork is often composed of tiny postage stamp-sized pieces of cotton in riotous combinations of orange, white, purple, yellow, red, green, pink and blue. The designers of these patchworks rarely use fewer than four colours. Favourite subjects are local flowers, butterflies and birds. A hexagonal representation of a turtle shell recurs often, or they may portray geometric and abstract designs very like the repeated images in a kaleidoscope, or multi-coloured mosaics of stars and crosses. Most are beautifully worked but could not be called elegant — at best they exhibit a jaunty vulgarity, and at worst a breathtaking and unashamed kitsch, as for example in the exquisitely made piecework of two highly carnivorous-looking red, yellow, pink and green Alsatian dogs grinning at each other. Fine handsewing is valued, but machine sewing is not despised and is much quicker: quilts made for the tourist trade tend to be sewn by machine.

The appliqué quilts are very different. They benefit from simple but dramatic colour schemes — often only two colours, red and white being favourites — and from strong symmetrical central motifs, cut from a sheet of paper folded in four in the Society Islands, and eight in Hawaii. Design expertise is revered among the Polynesians, and it is considered bad luck to repeat designs – often the pattern is destroyed after it has been used. The Cook Islands specialize in appliqué embellished with elaborate embroidered details.

There is a possibility of a finer, more delicate Hawaiian tradition which pre-dates the missionary-influenced style of bold appliquéd silhouettes that bear a strong resemblance to the leaf and flower designs stencilled on to barkcloth in Fiji. Originally in Hawaii much finer all-over block printing was used to decorate the cloth, the earliest example of which was collected by Captain Cook in 1779. But there was much trade among the islands and the Hawaiians may well have admired the design expertise of the Fijians and copied their strong motifs.

The finished quilts are used as wedding, farewell or funeral gifts, and imply great respect and devotion on the part of the giver. They are also hung up to give an area a ceremonial aspect for weddings or in feast houses.

RIGHT: *Inspired by the exotic local foliage and flowers, this early twentieth century Hawaiian appliqué quilt is padded with cotton and beautifully quilted in concentric waves around and within the white motif. Other boldly contrasting colours were often used in Hawaiian quilts, but nothing beats scarlet and white.*

RIGHT: *An unusual quilt with a stylized border of foliage, dignified by the title 'Maile lei', and a binding trim. Fine concentric lines of quilting hold the heavy wadding in place around the central design of 'Queen Kapiolani's fan' alternating with flowers.*

HAWAIIAN APPLIQUÉ WALL-HANGING

The classic combination of red and white in an extrovert quilted hanging. Few styles beat Hawaiian for simply achieved impact. The fine concentric rows of quilting are given texture by an interlining of cotton bump (curtain interlining), and the whole dramatic abstract composition is neatly contained within a scarlet frame.

THE HAWAIIANS HAVE a charming legend to explain the origin of their quilts. A woman noticed the attractive fretted shadow cast on the ground by leaves from a tree, so she traced the shape on to a piece of cloth, cut round it and sewed it to another cloth, thus creating the first Hawaiian quilt. Naturalism has never been the aim, however, and from the first vibrant greens, oranges, reds or bright prints were used, with a plain contrasting background. Alone among Polynesian quilts, Hawaiian textiles are quilted over wadding. Elsewhere, just two layers of cotton are used.

Traditionally, the quilting design radiates outwards from the central design in simple concentric waves. Alternatively, it may be stitched according to the classic British repertoire; it may take local patterns as inspiration — shells, fish scales, fishing nets or turtle shells, for example — or the indigenous barkcloth designs may resurface in regular geometric stitching patterns.

--- SHOPPING LIST ---

Several sheets medium-weight
paper, 28 in/71 cm square
Bondaweb: 2 yd/1 m 80 cm
Cotton bump (curtain interlining)
45 in/115 cm wide: 1yd/90 cm
White cotton 36 in/90 cm wide:
2½ yd/1 m 80cm
Red cotton 36 in/90 cm wide:
1¼ yd/1 m 15 cm
Cotton thread in red and white

There are certain traditions for the central motif: flowers, fruit, legends and Bible stories are illustrated over and over again in bold simplified silhouette. And there are the evocative abstract subjects of which the Hawaiians are fond: 'The wind that wafts love from one to another' is one. The classic repertoire has been increased by new-fangled and unfamiliar subjects such as paraffin lamps, anchors, crowns and fans. On completion, the pattern may be destroyed by its creator, anxious to keep it a one-off. People are also loath to have their quilts photographed, fearing they may be copied.

No matter what strange anachronistic objects find their way into quilt design, and what changes sewing machines may bring, Hawaiian women place great value on their quilts as a vital and continuing part of their cultural and personal identity. The cry of a Rarotongan woman echoes all over the islands of Polynesia: 'If I did not have any *tifaifai* (quilts), I would not be a woman!'

THE PALETTE
Plain white and red.

ALTERNATIVE DESIGNS

Finished wall-hanging measures approx. 32 × 32 in/81 × 81 cm.

Use template on page 122 or experiment with different designs of your own (see left for examples).

MAKING THE WALL-HANGING

1 *Fold piece of paper 28 in/71 cm square precisely in half, then half again to make a smaller square, and then again to make a triangle. The folds must be precise. Transfer design to folded paper (use template pattern on page 122 or experiment for yourself). The centre can be held firmly in position with staples. Cut neatly with a scalpel. Remove staples. Iron template flat.*

2 *Iron Bondaweb to cover back of 30 in/76 cm square of red cotton. Lightly spray template with adhesive and lay squarely on Bondaweb. Trace around edges with a soft pencil.*

3 *Cut out design. Use Olfa cutter for long cuts and small sharp scissors for difficult corners.*

4 *Fold white backing fabric 36 in/90 cm square in quarters and press to form guide lines. Bond to cotton bump with spray adhesive (see page 125). Peel away backing paper and bond red pattern to right side of white fabric, aligning along diagonals.*

5 *Zig-zag around all raw edges with red cotton in needle and white in bobbin. Adjust tension so that no bobbin thread shows on top of work.*

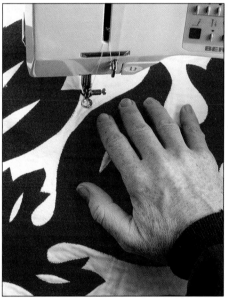

6 *Attach backing cloth to back of bump with spray adhesive (see page 125). Thread needle with white. Lower feed dog and, using darning foot, 'shadow quilt' white areas with all-over pattern (see page 125).*

7 *Rethread needle with red. Quilt red areas, following contours of design.*

8 *Trim excess fabric from edges to make a neat square. Pull threads to back and darn invisibly.*

9 *Cut 3 in/75 mm strips of red fabric, join, and attach all around quilt on wrong side. Fold over and secure with fine zig-zag stitches (see instructions for making and attaching binding on page 126).*

IRISH CHAIN QUILT

KNOWN IN AMERICA as Irish chain, and in Ireland as American chain, this very simple design is most commonly seen in the British Isles in the classic colour combination of Turkey red, pale green and white, which were produced for the first time with reliably colourfast dyes in the nineteenth century.

Nobody knows for sure where this simple and appealing block design originated, though blocks are characteristic of American quilts and do not feature so much in those of the British Isles. In America, the pattern was one of the oldest — simple squares transmuting into chains and double chains — and there are several dating from the early 1800s. There are a number from the 1870s in Ireland and the west of England.

It is a natural for machine piecing, although sewing machines were not common in Ireland until this century. Back in the 1830s, simple quilt-making was a source of revenue for the needy rural population, and children were put to work piecing quilts that could be exchanged for goods from the estate shops of the wealthy — the Duke of Manchester in Armagh kept his tenants fed and clothed in this way. Thrifty needlewomen kept a quilting frame in constant operation, slung on pulleys from the ceiling and ready to be used at a moment's notice.

Like the Americans, the Irish expected quilting to be a social activity. Quilting parties were a welcome event in rural winters. The earlier parties, known as frolics, were the best fun: they were attended by eligible young men, alcoholic drinks enlivened the atmosphere, and occasionally the charm of some young lady delicately plying her needle proved so overwhelming that proposals of marriage were made. But in time, religion and temperance took their toll, and in America especially quilting bees became very sober affairs.

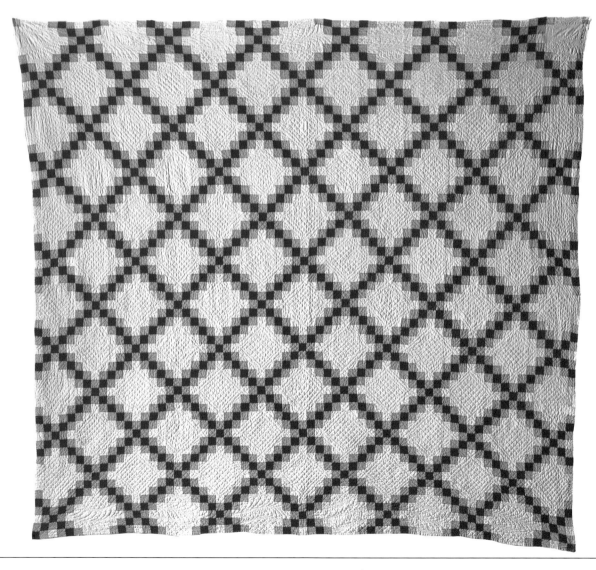

ABOVE: *The simple colour combination of red and white in a double Irish chain quilt from Ireland. Whether the quilts were taken to America by the Irish, or originated there and found their way back to Ireland is a moot point and the subject of fierce debate.*

LEFT: *A large late nineteenth century double Irish chain quilt from North Shields, Northumberland. A nicely faded and worn version in the popular combination of Turkey red, green and white which has obviously seen several dedicated generations of use. The centre is filled with diamond quilting, and two of the borders are 'running feather' pattern.*

RIGHT: *A Mennonite version of the double Irish chain pattern, using brilliant red and green on white. Enclosing the whole is a lively diamond border, which gives a somewhat jagged appearance to the white squares. On close scrutiny, you will find a mistake which may just have been put there intentionally as an expression of human fallibility.*

IRISH CHAIN QUILT

A simple patchwork design, using nothing more complicated than the basic square block, but put together with a cool mastery of colour to make a stylish quilt. In subtle contrast to Britain's popular red and green and Amish brights, this double chain in terracotta and grey pays homage to one of the oldest patterns and lends itself to speedy machining.

ONE OF THE oldest quilt designs and often the first project attempted by the novice quilter, Irish chain looks more demanding to make than it is. It consists of just two basic blocks which can be worked individually until the thrilling moment when the whole thing is put together and the bold chequerboard is seen in all its glory. Single Irish chain is the most basic variant, using just one colour against white in a simple diagonal lattice. Double Irish chain is made up of chains three blocks wide with the central one traditionally in a lighter colour. Triple Irish chain is five blocks wide and generally made from three different colours against white calico. Plain colours were traditionally purchased with an eye to harmony, although occasionally the design became a rainbow of ragbag pieces. In the past, quilters would demonstrate their expertise by using tiny 1 in/25 mm squares, but fortunately the design works equally well boldly pieced in more manageable 2 in/50 mm squares.

The Amish and Mennonites used their rich and typical colours to give Irish chain a quite different rose-window glow, with stronger background colours like cerise with blue and green chains, or sand with scarlet and royal blue, or even the startling primary contrast of bright yellow diagonals on a Prussian blue background. Their quilts tended to have more finely stitched decorative quilting, with plaits and waves showing up well on the plain fabric.

Among dedicated quilters, variations on the simple pattern developed in time — 'puss in a corner' uses differing square sizes in clusters at the crossings to give a rather restless and busy finish; 'Burgoyne surrounded' is a more complicated permutation of large square blocks encircled with smaller blocks at the points where the diagonals cross. The name refers to an incident in the American Revolutionary War when the British were forced to surrender. Not surprisingly it does not appear much in British quilt collections.

SHOPPING LIST

When choosing material make sure that grey print is darker in tone than terracotta.

Cotton and cotton prints 45 in/115 cm wide:

Grey 1½ yd/1 m 40 cm

Plain terracotta 1 yd/90 cm

Natural off-white 2¼ yd/2 m 5 cm

Plain cotton (backing) 60 in/150 cm wide: 2 yd/1 m 90 cm

Cotton bump (curtain interlining) 60 in/150 cm wide: 2 yd/1 m 80 cm

Invisible nylon thread

Cotton thread to match back and binding

THE PALETTE
One dark grey print, plus plain terracotta and off-white.

THE COMPONENTS

Finished quilt measures approx. 46 × 61 in/117 × 155 cm.

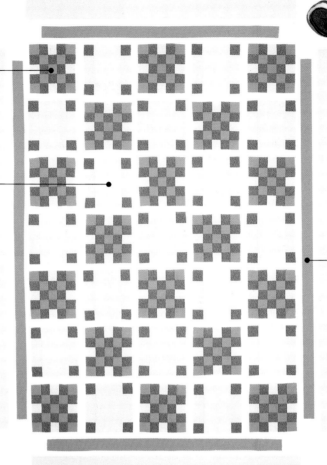

CHEQUERBOARD SQUARES: 18, made of 5 strips of squares, each 2 in/ 50 mm wide, in 3 different permutations.

GREY-CORNERED SQUARES: 17, made by sewing grey-tipped strips 2 in/50 cm wide to either side of an off-white rectangle 5 × 8 in/13 × 20.5 cm.

BINDING: Grey print strips 3 in/75 mm wide. Join and prepare as on page 126.

FIRST BORDER: 4 strips terracotta 2 in/50 mm wide (join where necessary), cut to size (top and bottom pieces to extend over side pieces).

SECOND BORDER: 4 strips off-white 5 in/ 13 cm wide (join where necessary), cut to size (top and bottom pieces to extend over side pieces).

MAKING THE QUILT

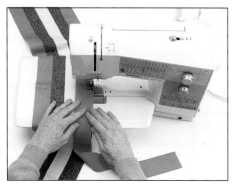

1 Cut 2 in/ 50 mm wide strips across width of the three fabrics. Cut at least 9 terracotta strips, 16 grey print strips and 4 white strips.

2 Sew strips together lengthways with very accurate ¼ in/6 mm seams to make long striped pieces.

3 Terracotta, grey and white strips are sewn togther in 3 different combinations and then arranged in symmetrical groups of five to form the chequerboard squares. Sew 2 long T-G-W-G-T and G-T-G-T-G strips, and one W-G-T-G-W strip. Press all grey seams outwards. Cut across the stripes to make 2 in/50 mm wide strips: Cut 36 T-G-W-G-T pieces, 36 G-T-G-T-G pieces and 18 W-G-T-G-W pieces.

4 *Cut 2 strips white 5 in/13 cm wide. Sew 2 remaining grey strips either side. Cut 34 pieces 2 in/50 mm wide.*

5 *Cut 17 white pieces 5 × 8 in/13 × 20.5 cm. Arrange blocks as shown.*

6 *Piece together chequerboard blocks, carefully lining up seams and using a ¼ in/6 mm seam. Press.*

7 *Piece together grey-cornered blocks using a ¼ in/6 mm seam. Press.*

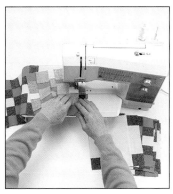

8 *Sew alternating blocks together to form rows as shown in exploded diagram.*

9 *Sew rows together and press all seams.*

10 *Attach borders of terracotta and white (see step 8 for Amish Cot Quilt, page 37).*

11 *Attach back and wadding (p. 125). Draw lines on white patches with water-erasable pen. Quilt along these and all seams with invisible thread (p. 125).*

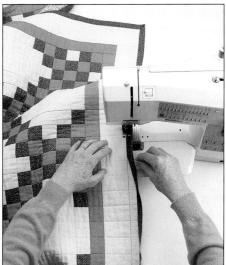

12 *For binding, cut strips of grey 3 in/75 mm wide, fold in four and attach (see page 126).*

13 *Remove lines of water-erasable pen by spraying with water.*

JAPANESE SASHIKO CUSHION

◆

THE CLEAN, UNCLUTTERED precision of Japanese sashiko quilting — the name means little stabs — goes back to the early 1800s when the men whose outdoor work forced them to battle with the rigours of a snowbound Japanese winter — woodcutters, fishermen and farmers — protected themselves by wearing quilted cotton jackets. Originally the tight, plain little running stitch also kept together the loosely woven fibres of hemp, linen, paper-mulberry bark or grasses which were the raw materials of most textiles until the introduction of cotton. Silk, introduced in the fifth century AD by Korean weavers, was only for the very wealthy.

Extreme cold was one incentive for the invention of thick warm fabric; so was heat. Firemen found that closely quilted padded jackets held flames at bay, particularly when they were soaked in water, and the padding dulled the impact of falling cinders and timber. The quilting on firemen's coats is usually very simple, consisting of close-set rows of running stitches, but the linings were often emblazoned with vigorous paintings of heroes, carp — the symbol of courage and success — or phoenixes, which bring peace and prosperity, to encourage the wearer to feats of bravery. On ceremonial occasions the coats were turned inside-out and the firemen, who were rightly revered for their vital role in a country of densely packed wooden houses, paraded their icons. Samurai warriors also wore 'kendo' coats — sashiko-stitched jackets used in fencing practice and lovingly toiled over by their wives and mothers.

Sashiko stitching had another use — this was in the making of panelled 'hiyuoke noren', or 'door curtains', which often hung outside shops and houses. Typically these were dyed indigo or brown, which are both relatively colourfast, and acted both as draught excluders and screens, allowing a modicum of privacy in lieu of proper doors. Sashiko also played a part in the ubiquitous tea ceremony, the precious accoutrements of which were tenderly laid in ceremonial protective wrapping cloths when not in use — these are dignified by the name 'meibutsugire', 'wrappings for famous objects'. 'Fukusa', square cloths used to wrap gifts, are also occasionally embellished with sashiko stitching. At one time there was a royal prohibition on the use of bright colours among commoners, as a result of which the classic combination for any but the most regal textiles is indigo and white.

City dwellers took up the art of sashiko stitching which, as a result, became ever more sophisticated, until the 1930s when interest in this tradition disappeared altogether, to be resuscitated in a very genteel form twenty years later.

LEFT: *A fireman's jacket, combining fine stitch-work on the sleeves with a hand-printed design symbolizing water. Often, these splendid garments had very decorative linings and were reversed on ceremonial occasions. The coats were soaked in water to confer greater heat and flame resistance.*

RIGHT: *The ultimate in samurai elegance, a beautifully hand-stitched nineteenth century 'kendo' coat. Intended to be worn during fencing practice, such coats were made as a labour of love by the sisters, wives and mothers of the warriors.*

LEFT: *A nineteenth century coat stitched in white on heavy deep-dyed indigo cotton. This purely decorative stitching, 'kogin', was a speciality of the Tsugaru district of the western Aomori prefecture and originated as a way of creating warm quilted garments from loosely woven fibres.*

JAPANESE SASHIKO CUSHION

◆

The simplest stitches used to elegant effect. Bold white sashiko quilting against the classic background of indigo cotton demonstrates perfectly the Japanese art of creating something beautiful out of the most basic materials. In contrast, the dashes of cinnabar red in the tassels, along with their silkiness, add a touch of colour and luxury to the cushion.

THE JAPANESE ARE masters of the art of the minimal. Many of their classic designs for ceramics, textiles and architecture date from a period of high refinement in the sixteenth century and remain almost unchanged. Sashiko has a long history as a hard-wearing textile — originally the technique was a purely practical method of strengthening loosely woven fibres and binding them together. But as time went by, the utilitarian nature of the stitches was forgotten and gradually the designs were refined, tracing elegant variations on traditional kimono prints, or taking inspiration from nature in plants, tortoise shells or the swelling waves of the sea. Hemp leaves and flowers, flowers-in-diamonds, persimmon flowers, bamboo fences and baskets, pointed blue ocean waves, pampas grass blowing in the wind, the seven treasures of Buddha are all poetic sashiko patterns familiar to any enthusiast.

------ SHOPPING LIST ------

To make 2 cushions
Close-woven indigo cotton
45 in/115 cm wide: 2¼ yd/
2 m 5 cm
Thick soft fabric such as flannel
(backing) 45 in/115 cm wide:
1½ yd/1 m 40 cm
Embroidery thread (DMC
stranded cotton), white and red
(DMC no. 5): 1 skein each
2 24 in/60 cm feather-filled
cushion pads or loose stuffing
Cotton thread to match indigo
White tacking thread and
tailor's chalk

The 'hanten', a stylish and practical straight full-sleeved coat, became the excuse for creating a sample of quilting virtuosity which was brought to a peak of perfection in the Tohoku district of northern Honshu, a place well accustomed to prolonged sub-zero winters with copious amounts of snow.

The filling for quilted garments was usually cotton wadding or layers of cotton quilted together to produce a texture that was stiff and ridged. The Japanese also used to have a partiality for paper which gave a little rain and wind resistance and made a comforting rustling sound. Wool has never been much of a success in Japan, and sheep are few and far between.

Typically the decoration is done with special undyed thick cotton, around six stitches to the inch. The stitching is regular and rhythmical, forming stars at the intersections of the design.

THE PALETTE
Plain indigo, plus red stranded cotton for tassels and white to quilt.

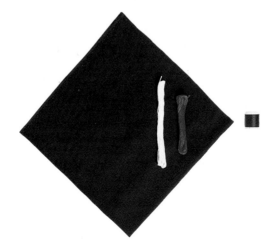

ALTERNATIVE DESIGNS

Finished cushion measures approx. 24 × 24 in/61 × 61 cm.

*Use chrysanthemum template on page 123 or experiment
with different geometric patterns of your own (see above for examples).*

MAKING THE CUSHION

1 *Cut 25 in/64 cm square of blue cotton and backing material. Tack together round edges. Mark centre by folding vertically and horizontally and tack along folds. Mark out a centred 16 in/41 cm square.*

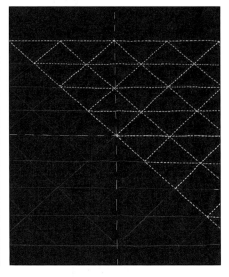

2 *For geometric design, mark 4 in/10 cm intervals around square. Draw quilting lines diagonally and horizontally as shown or mark with narrow masking tape.*

3 *Thread needle with 4 strands of white DMC cotton and stitch along all lines.*

4 *For chrysanthemum design, cut cushion top and wadding and mark vertical and horizontal lines as in step 1. Make a template out of stiff card for the chrysanthemum shape using the outline on page 123. Trace around template with tailor's chalk, in two diagonally opposite squares. Quilt as before.*

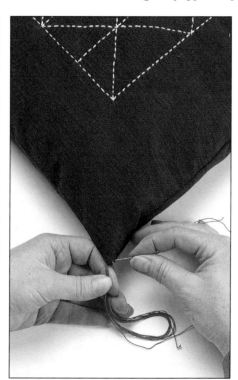

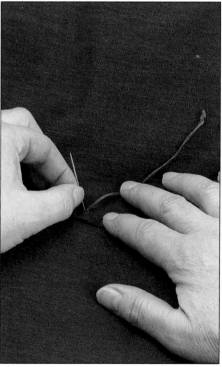

5 *Cut two pieces of blue cotton 25×14½ in/64×37 cm and 25×19½ in/64×50 cm. Hem each piece. Place on top of cushion top, right sides facing, with hemmed edges overlapping in centre. Pin all round, and stitch ½ in/13 mm from edge. Zig-zag around raw edges, turn cushion right side out and insert pad. If using loose stuffing, sew up opening. Repeat for second cushion.*

6 *To make corner tassels, thread needle with a long piece of red embroidery thread. Sew 8 loops 4 in/10 cm long, tie knot close to corner and trim tassel.*

7 *For centre tassel, wind red thread 8 times around your spread fingers, tie and trim. Thread long needle with double thread and stitch through cushion. Catch tassel, return thread to back and tie ends.*

Japanese Yogi Quilt

Like many thrifty rural cultures, the Japanese valued textiles, and kimonos, padded and recycled as yogi quilts, came about as the most economic way to make a garment from a bolt of woven cloth. The standard strip of woven cloth measured about 14 in/ 35 cm wide and 12 yd/11m long, dimensions dictated by the draw loom on which it was woven. Home-grown linen was the usual cloth for all but the nobility until the eighteenth century, when cotton prevailed and grew well in the south. Indigo was the usual dye, and was believed to confer immunity to snake-bites. A single dip of the cloth into the dye resulted in a very pale blue, dignified with the term 'kame-nozoki', meaning 'a peep into the dye vat'. Twenty immersions gave a rich blue-black material called 'kachi-iro' or 'victory colour' by the optimistic samurai warriors who wore it.

The long narrow piece of cloth was cut and sewn simply: two strips to make the back, one each side plus a narrow strip and binding for the fronts, and a strip for each sleeve. The whole thing is carefully calculated and constructed from long narrow rectangles, and not a single scrap of fabric is left over at the end. Like many Japanese artefacts, the kimono is a triumph of beauty and economy. Weaving and needlework were traditionally highly esteemed and religious festivals pay homage to the importance of these skills to everyday life — Tanabata on 7 July is the festival of the Weaving Maid, and Hari Kuyo is an annual pilgrimage to a Shinto shrine. Devotees offer bent and broken needles and pins in the hope that the following year will bring successful stitching.

Everybody used to wear kimonos, and they were recycled in many different guises. From being ceremonial best they became everyday garments. In the next trans-formation they were shortened to make jackets or padded and used as sleepsuits or quilts (yogis). Like many natural fabrics coloured with plant dyes, most Japanese fabrics improve with time, and people are reluctant to throw away even a tiny beautiful scrap, so further evolution saw the original kimono becoming carrying cloths or bags, then aprons, and the final farewell diminished the glorious garment into humble but evocative dusters.

Sashiko quilting was one way of prolonging the use-ful life of a kimono, since stitching to a strong backing fabric held worn fabric together, and a useful side-effect was warmth gained in the layering of cloth. Yogi quilts take this discovery a stage further by intentionally using thick cotton wadding, stitched quite loosely to trap warm air within the covers.

LEFT: *A nineteenth century yogi featuring a family crest and a design of pine and bamboo, signifying strength, flexibility and longevity. Rice paste squeezed through a funnel was used to make the resist design.*

BELOW: *Nothing Japanese is without symbolism; this design of 'noshi' – dried bundles of abalone – was considered highly auspicious. The yogi, or quilted coat, was used as an all-enveloping bed-covering, being thickly padded and over six feet long.*

LEFT: *A nineteenth century yogi bearing a family crest and paulownia blossom. The skill of the designer and the fabric printer is apparent in the matching of the design and the fluidity of the hand-printing.*

JAPANESE YOGI QUILT

Indigo and white cotton is here put together in a crisp chequerboard design familiar from traditional kimonos, and thickly padded to withstand the iciest of winter chills. The lining of resist-dyed cotton is embellished with a huge hand-printed idiogram promising sweet dreams, and the binding is brightly striped with scarlet.

THE JAPANESE HAVE a talent for perfection. The stencil designs, known as 'katazome', which are characteristic of much indigo and white cotton or silk, are intricate and highly symbolic. Soaring falcons, angular flying cranes, plum blossom, bamboo, the familiar cone of Mount Fuji, whiskered carp in bubbling streams, even dried abalone strips have auspicious connotations, but it is their beauty that makes them classics. Some of the more ambitious designs were stencilled on to the finished garment. The stencils themselves used to be cut from sixteen layers of paper gathered from the paper-mulberry tree, stiffened with date plum juice and oil, and stuck together in pairs enclosing a fine web of human hair to keep the stencil from distorting or tearing. The cloth was then painted with a resist, and dipped in the dye vat.

As well as the giant chequerboard pattern I have used, the Japanese sometimes

used a finer patchwork of sumptuous fabrics in their kimonos, consisting of long straight strips. The symbolic significance was that as patches prolong the life of a garment, so wearing this motley 'dofuku' would bring longevity to its owner. Even the number of patches may have auspicious meaning.

Japanese quilts evolved from thick padded kimonos which were worn to sleep in, sometimes in several layers to keep out the cold of bitter snowbound nights in draughty wooden houses where the only heating was a central wood-burning stove, and the only mattress a futon — a kind of thick cotton-stuffed quilt — on the tatami-matting floor. The quilts retained their characteristic kimono shape, and the thick wadding was held in place by large basting stitches in white thread, and occasional knots. This meant that the whole thing could be dismantled for washing.

SHOPPING LIST

3 indigo-print kimonos or cotton fabric 45 in/115 cm wide:

Dark print 2 yd/1m 80 cm

2 lighter prints 1 yd/90 cm each

Red-striped fabric (binding) 45 in/115 cm wide: 1 yd/90 cm

Plain indigo fabric (backing) 45 in/115 cm wide: 2¼ yd/2 m 5 cm

8 oz Terylene wadding 60 in/ 150 cm wide: 4½ yd/4 m

2 skeins of soft embroidery cotton (not stranded)

Cotton thread to match indigo

THE PALETTE
Three contrasting indigo and white prints, plus indigo and red stripe for binding.

THE COMPONENTS

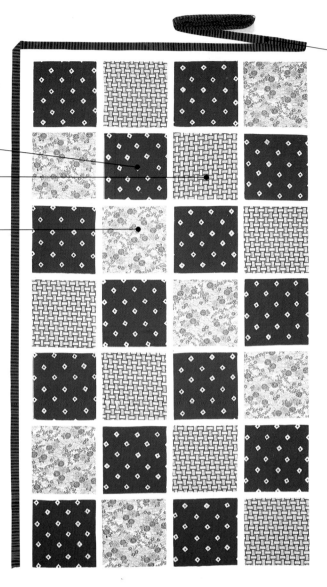

*Finished quilt measures approx.
46 × 80 in/115 × 200 cm.*

*BINDING: Red-striped strips
6 in/15 cm wide. Join and
prepare as on page 126.*

*14 12 in/30 cm squares dark
indigo print.*

*7 12 in/30 cm squares light
indigo geometric print.*

*7 12 in/30 cm squares light
indigo floral print.*

MAKING THE QUILT

1 *Make a template of thick card 12 in/30 cm square. Cut 14
squares of dark print, 7 squares each of both lighter prints.*

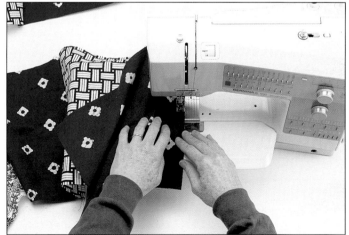

2 *Sew squares together in rows according to exploded
view. Remember to use ¼ in/6 mm seams at all times,
otherwise the finished rows will not align. Press seams towards
darker squares.*

3 *Sew rows together, matching seams. Cut back and wadding slightly larger than top. Press quilt top and assemble using sticky wadding method (see page 125).*

4 *Tack layers together at edges and zig-zag to secure.*

5 *Trim away excess material to edge of quilt top.*

6 *Pin through all layers at centre of each square, measuring to mark centres.*

7 *Turn the quilt over and work on the reverse side. Use masking tape stretched between pins along length of quilt as stitching guide.*

8 *Quilt from back to front with 1½ in/ 40 mm long stitches.*

9 *Join lengths of cotton with double knots. Cut ends to 1 in/25 mm.*

10 *Viewed from the front, the stitches are very small.*

11 *Cut 6 in/15 cm wide binding strips. Join strips together, fold and press (finished binding is 1½ in/40 mm wide) and attach (see page 126).*

PAKISTANI TASSELLED QUILT

I NDIA, PARTICULARLY THE north-west, is the place to visit for textiles and has been so from the dawn of documentation. Dyed and woven cloth from the third millennium BC has been discovered near the Indus river. Cotton grows wild here, and it was probably first cultivated in Sind, Pakistan. Subsequently, the combined art of sophisticated dyeing and intricate block printing, producing brilliant and subtle colours and designs, made Indian cloth much coveted and imitated. It is thought that the familiar word 'chintz' derives from the Hindi word for 'variegated' — 'chint' — referring to printed calico painted with a fixative mordant. Indian textiles were much prized, and were exported to Japan and Africa as well as Europe and America. The techniques eventually spread from India to Persia and then to Turkey, where similar fabrics were produced more cheaply.

However, the Indian originals still retained their cachet, so much so that from the seventeenth century import of Indian printed fabrics was forbidden in Great Britain, France and America in order to foster home production — a prohibition which had the predictable effect of encouraging smuggling, so strong was the fashionable passion for the delicious forbidden goods. Walls were covered in painted Indian cloth showing exotic flora and fauna, and patterned and bordered palampores embellished the beds of the wealthy.

What put printed Indian fabrics in a class of their own for centuries was the extraordinary richness of the colours, allied with the technical expertise in the use of mordants which fixed the colours to make them, at the time, uniquely colourfast. Additionally, Indian wood-block printers were the envy of the world. They could not be emulated in the West, however, until the cunning secrets of using mordants had been purloined by industrial espionage. The complexities of over-printing or painting the dye with mordant were incomprehensible until the East India Company had sent out their spies — like the Frenchman Antoine de Beaulieu who visited the print workshops in Pondicherry and reported home with the formulae in the mid-eighteenth century. In the nineteenth century the process was mechanized, and great rollers printed the designs — resulting in much quicker production and requiring minimal skill on the part of the workforce.

ABOVE: *A Cholistani version of Irish chain, appliquéd with motifs derived from ancient geometric formulae.*

ABOVE RIGHT: *A fine patchwork ralli from Sind, Pakistan, tasselled, intricately bordered and interlined with scraps.*

RIGHT: *An intricate appliquéd ralli from Hyderabad, Pakistan, in earth and spice colours.*

FAR RIGHT: *The 'flying geese' pattern in exotic guise, made in Sind, Pakistan, in the 1960s.*

PAKISTANI TASSELLED QUILT

A quilt in traditional red, yellow, black, green and white — dramatic pinwheels of strong colour redolent of spice markets and a sun-baked landscape, finished with chunky scarlet tassels. The bright plain cottons are aged in tea for a more subdued and antique look, in imitation of an effect that only years of heat and dust can achieve.

BRIGHT GEOMETRIC INDIAN and Pakistan patchwork quilts are known as rallies (sometimes rillies), a word derived from the Urdu meaning 'to mix' or 'connect'. The tradition of making them is still current, from Baluchistan, through Sind, to Rajasthan, Gujerat and Kutch. Their most striking feature is their bold colouring, laden with symbolic meaning — saffron yellow, for example, recalls the earth, and red betokens love. Originally the dyes came from natural sources — red from madder roots mixed with other plants to give varying degrees of brightness; turmeric and myrobalan flowers yielded the familiar rich yellow; indigo overdyed with yellow produced green.

The most common quilts, with their prevalent geometric motifs, hark back to a time before the Islamic invasion, with its fondness for flowers and fancy decoration. Many of the pieced quilt designs come from Central Asia, deriving from Sun worship symbols (the omnipresent quincunx of five squares symbolic of welcome and protection, for example), and they still have religious nuances — the devotees of the Pir (religious leader) are wont to present the most beautiful quilts to him as gifts. They are also used as hangings to lend gravitas to a meeting place for ceremonial purposes.

They are made by women, and every community has its local tradition for colour and pattern, although sadly the whole industry is dying out. They are used for everything: throwing over the back of a horse or camel for the saddle to rest upon; as mattresses; as seating in courtyards; and for vast crowds visiting a shrine during a religious festival, where the families all picnic on them. Looking inside a house, your eyes will very likely be met by a ziggurat of fifty quilts stacked in a perfect pyramid, the whole thing covered by the most beautiful quilt of all to greet the eye of the visitor.

The women make summer quilts, and also winter ones (with up to six layers of cotton cloth within). Everything is recycled, and inside a hefty winter quilt will very likely be the tattered remains of one or two old summer quilts along with fabric of all sorts for padding. However, their creators choose only the best, often specially bought cloth for the outside.

SHOPPING LIST

Medium-weight cotton 45 in/
115 cm wide:

Red 1 yd/90 cm

Yellow ¾ yd/70 cm

Black 1¾ yd/1 m 60 cm

White 1¼ yd/1 m 15 cm

Green ¾ yd/70 cm

The fabric may be aged by dipping
in tea

Indian block-printed
medium-weight cotton paisley
tablecloth or bedspread at least
60 x 52 in/150 x 130 cm

Flannel sheet, brushed cotton or
thin blanket (interlining) at least
60 x 52 in/150 x 130 cm

Red 4-ply cotton knitting yarn
(tassels and tying)

Gold metallic thread (tassels)

THE PALETTE
Plain yellow, vermillion, green, white and black.

THE COMPONENTS

*Finished quilt measures approx.
53 × 60 in/135 × 152 cm.*

*Use RIT square
template on page 124.*

RED AND GREEN
WINDMILLS: *8, made
from 32 no. 2 RIT
squares in red and green.*

RED AND YELLOW
WINDMILLS: *7, made
from 28 no. 2 RIT
squares in red and yellow.*

BLACK AND WHITE
WINDMILLS:
*15, made from 60 no. 2
RIT squares in black
and white.*

TASSELS: *4 (see page
127).*

FIRST BORDER:
*4 strips black approx.
2½ in/65 mm wide
(join where necessary),
cut to size (top and
bottom pieces to extend
over side pieces).*

SECOND BORDER:
*4 strips white approx.
1¾ in/45 mm wide
(join where necessary),
cut to size (top and
bottom pieces to extend
over side pieces).*

THIRD BORDER:
*4 strips red approx.
1¼ in/30 mm wide
(join where necessary),
cut to size (top and
bottom pieces to extend
over side pieces).*

FOURTH BORDER:
*4 strips black approx.
3 in/75 mm wide
(join where necessary),
cut to size (top and
bottom pieces to extend
over side pieces).*

MAKING THE QUILT

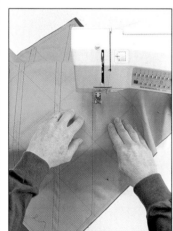

*1 Place red and yellow fabric
20 in/51 cm square
right sides together. Draw 14
squares using template on page
124, and parallel diagonal lines.
Sew ¼ in/6 mm seams either side
in red thread.*

*2 Cut along all drawn lines to
form 28 triangles. Press open
to make red and yellow squares
with seam pressed towards
darker colour.*

*3 Sew together in groups of 4 to make 7 pinwheels. In the same
way, make 8 red and green pinwheels (32 squares — draw 16)
and 15 black and white pinwheels (60 squares — draw 30).*

4 Sew pinwheels together to form rows, following layout in exploded diagram.

5 Sew rows together, matching seams and corners exactly. It is now that you appreciate the importance of being accurate and consistent in using a ¼ in/6 mm seam allowance. Precision is critical, otherwise seams and corners will not align. If you do run into problems, ease and stretch the material to fit, then press well.

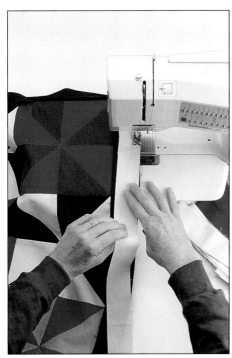

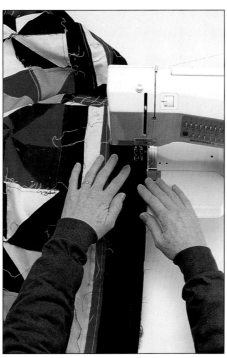

6 Attach borders as shown on layout (see step 8 for Amish Cot Quilt on page 37). Clip away bulky seams carefully and press well. Cut backing fabric and interlining the same size as quilt and machine tack them together. Sew quilt top to backing and interlining, right sides together, leaving an 18 in/46 cm opening down one side. Turn right side out, press thoroughly, and sew up opening. (This quilt has no binding.)

7 Make tassels (see page 127) and attach securely to corners of quilt.

PANAMANIAN MOLA WALL-HANGING

HE KUNA INDIANS inhabit about fifty of the 386 atolls in the San Blas archipelago off the Caribbean coast of Panama. The people create complex and unique appliqué designs similar in technique to the appliqué of the Hmong in Thailand. They are known as molas — 'mola' is the Kuna word for cloth — and are thought to be a continuation of an ancient practice of body painting and tattooing commented on by Lionell Wafer, an astounded traveller of 1681. Kuna women used to decorate their bodies and those of the men with brilliant primary dyes produced from tree bark, earth, plants and berries:

'The women are the painters and take great delight in it. The colours they like and use most are red, yellow and blue... they make figures of birds, beasts, men, trees or the like up and down in every part of the body, more especially the faces.'

The subject matter and colours have not changed, but the materials have. Initially cotton was grown and dyed locally, gathered and spun by daughters for their mothers to weave. They always wove exactly enough for the purpose — hammocks, skirts, tunics or blankets — so they did not need to cut the woven fabric.

The reverse appliqué technique was used in the past for tunics and skirt decoration and was simpler than the astonishing many-layered works of art that the women take such pride in now. Brilliant multi-coloured molas are made by the women as intricate panels for the front and back of their blouses, and men occasionally enliven their clothing with a touch of mola appliqué on waistcoats, collars, cuffs and pockets. Girls start sewing at the age of six, and by the time they marry will have made about twenty blouses, cartoon characters and advertising logos now added to the repertoire of more conventional motifs.

LEFT: *Two badges, one of a parrot, the other of a hermit crab, speedily, but still finely, stitched to satisfy the tourist trade.*

RIGHT: *A small piece of work, 8×6 in/20×15 cm, showing a rather Mayan-looking bird, a 'sikwi', reverse-appliquéd on to bright yellow cotton.*

BELOW LEFT: *Pipe-smoking parrots are not common in patchwork, but are typical of the Kuna fascination with jokey anthropomorphic animals.*

BELOW: *A gaggle of twenty of the familiar and favoured parrots, known as 'kwili', on a background of assorted 'nips' and 'pips'. Backed with maroon, the piece, which was taken from a blouse-front, measures 16×8½ in/40.5×21.5 cm.*

Panamanian Mola Wall-Hanging

A brilliant piece of virtuoso machine work, this mola depicts a nattily dressed cat. Complex and time-consuming (though much speedier than an authentic hand-stitched Kuna mola which takes up to two months to complete), it is a splendid example of extrovert ethnic-style décor, fit to be framed and displayed for universal admiration.

MOLAS ARE USUALLY rectangles measuring about 17 x 19 in/43 x 48 cm. They consist of a fabric foundation of two layers of strong cotton, often black, covered with several layers of lightweight cotton which are cut away to reveal the colours beneath then hemmed with invisible stitches. The characteristic lozenge-shaped slits are known as 'tastas', and the dots of colour on many molas are called 'nips' and 'pips' depending on whether they are holes cut from the upper fabric or tiny patches appliquéd on top. Different islands have developed variants of their own, such as the Ailigandi islanders in the east who just use two colours to produce something like the original 'mugan' or grandmother mola, and the Karti group who specialize in tiny 'nips' and 'pips'.

Fine details are worked in minute chain, cross, straight, buttonhole and couching stitches.

Molas can be abstract and regular, designed using folded paper cut-outs or showing complicated mazes. Usually, however, they depict people and animals, plants and fish or the corals that surround the islands. The Kuna keep up with the times and like to add such things as rockets, football or baseball images and even advertising slogans to their repertoire. Lettering has always been a favourite subject.

The usual colours are bright yellows, oranges, reds, purples, greens, Prussian blue, black and white. The top layer is almost invariably black, orange, scarlet or crimson. Recently there has been a fad for using pastel colours which have none of the impact of the traditional palette.

SHOPPING LIST

Good quality cotton 20 in/51 cm squares:

Orange

Red

Black

Green

Blue

Yellow

Heavyweight iron-on Vilene: 20 in/51 cm

Bondaweb: 2 yd/1 m 80 cm

Cotton thread to match red and black

Embroidery cotton in all colours plus white

THE PALETTE
Plain black, blue, green, yellow, orange and red.

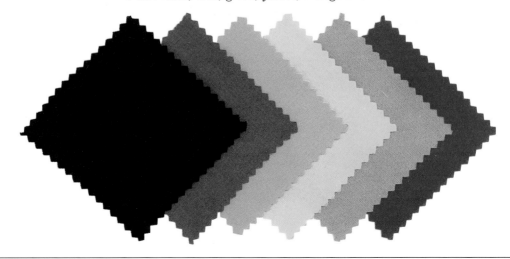

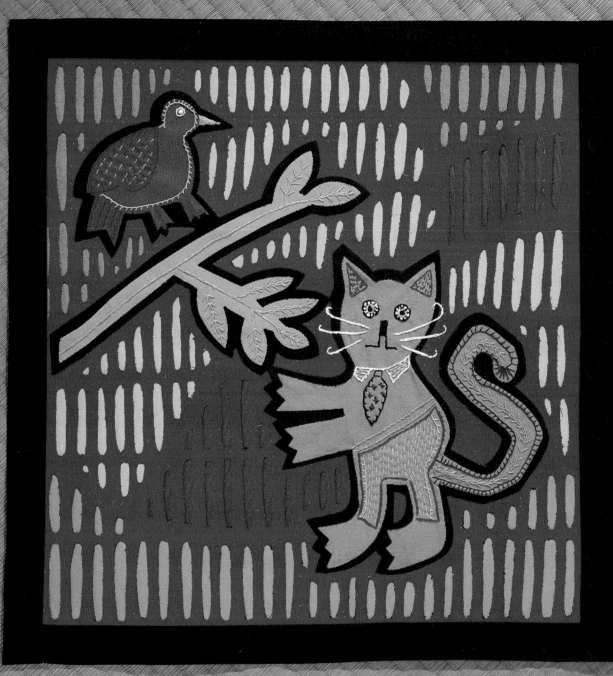

THE COMPONENTS

*Finished wall-hanging measures approx.
18 × 18 in/46 × 46 cm.*

*Bondaweb fixed to back of red and
black squares. Figures traced in
reverse on paper side of both squares
are cut out, paper removed and
red fixed to black.*

*BORDER: 4 strips black hemmed
cotton approx. 2 in/50 cm wide, cut to
size (top and bottom pieces to extend
over side pieces).*

*Heavyweight Vilene fixed to back of
orange square. Bondaweb fixed to back
of each background colour and shapes
cut out. Paper removed and
background shapes fixed to orange
square. Holes then cut through red and
black to reveal different colours, paper
removed from back of black and black
fixed to background.*

MAKING THE WALL-HANGING

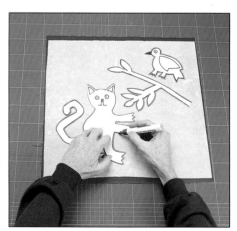

1 *Bond orange square to Vilene. Iron
Bondaweb to red, black, blue, green and
yellow. Trace around templates (see pages
122–3) on back of red with water-erasable
pen (min. ¹/₂ in/13 mm between elements).*

2 *Cut through Bondaweb and cloth with
scalpel, ¹/₄ in/6 mm outside traced line.*

3 *Centre right side of red on Bondaweb
side of black fabric. Centre the
templates within cut-out areas of red and
trace around edges.*

4 *Cut through paper and black cloth exactly on traced lines.*

5 *Lay red fabric face-up on black. Check that there is a ¼ in/6 mm margin of black showing. Peel paper from Bondaweb on back of red.*

6 *Carefully bond red to black with iron, taking care to keep the pieces in alignment and not stretch the material.*

7 *Using glass marking pencil, carefully trace furthest (red) outline of the figures on to two pieces of acetate. Cut one to make templates for background areas. Keep the other as a placement guide.*

8 *Use these templates to draw outlines on right side of orange to act as guide for positioning. Select colours and trace carefully around patterns in reverse on Bondaweb paper side of chosen colour.*

9 *Cut out all background colour pieces. Position them on orange fabric so they do not overlap and so the cut-out areas of red and black pieces are entirely covered. Check by overlaying red and black pieces.*

10 *When everything is correctly positioned, peel off backing paper (except red and black piece) and bond colours to orange with iron. The cat shape will remain orange.*

11 *Overlay acetate tracing on red fabric, holding in place with clips. Lift sheet and mark lines between colour areas on red with water-erasable pen.*

12 *Draw regular lozenge shapes on red within colour areas with water-erasable pen. Cut them with a scalpel. When laid on the bonded fabrics these holes will reveal different colours beneath.*

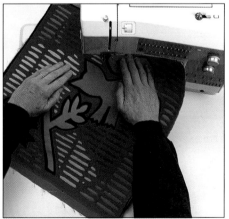

13 *Set stitch width to 1.5 and use red cotton. Lower feed dog and zig-zag around all raw edges of red fabric with darning foot. Repeat with matching colours on all raw edges.*

14 *Decorate figures with hand or machine embroidery. Cut black borders 1¾ in/45 mm wide and attach to wall-hanging (see step 8 for Amish Cot Quilt on page 37).*

SEMINOLE INDIAN CUSHION

THE INDIANS WHO are now known as Seminole are 'the Unconquerables'. They are the survivors of several tribes — the Muskhogean tribe of the Creek Indians from Alabama and Georgia formed a large percentage of them, along with the Mikasuki, and Cherokee, the Choctaw and the Chicasaw — routed and dispersed by President Andrew Jackson following his brutal Indian Removal Act of 1830. The word 'simanole' was initially a Creek word for runaway or separatist, referring to the tribesmen who were evicted from their homelands. In 1843, after seven years of battle with government troops, they were driven into the furthest and most inhospitable corners of the Florida Everglades.

Despite the displacement and near genocide of the indigenous population caused by European settlers, vestiges of art and culture remain in all sorts of guises, combining elements of tradition with modern touches. The Indians of North America have long been legendary for their skill in the universal crafts of pottery, basketwork, weaving, woodwork and their prowess with more arcane materials such as feathers, porcupine quills, sealion whiskers and abalone shells. In the areas of textiles, the strong stripes and chevrons of Pueblo and Navajo weaving are well known and much admired. The Apache still make bold cloth appliqué, and like the Seminole they have a passion for ric-rac with which they embellish clothing and saddlebags. The Lake and Prairie Indians are masters of the sophisticated art of ribbon appliqué.

With the advent of the sewing machine around 1900, the Florida Indians were spurred to create something totally original: a kaleidoscope of rainbow-pieced patterns unlike anything to be found elsewhere. They made, and continue to make, the brilliant striped textiles into billowing long skirts for women, which are worn with plain off-the-shoulder cape blouses, and generous 'big shirts' for the men.

LEFT: *A woman's silk cape and brilliant confetti-patterned skirt, typical of Mikasuki Seminole costume between 1930 and 1950. The quality of the workmanship is astounding, a startling tribute to the simple hand-operated sewing machine without which Seminole patchwork could never have evolved.*

RIGHT: *A man's shirt, dating from the 1960s. The 'big shirt' has been diminished to a ghost of its original glory, and rows of ric-rac have been applied to achieve a lively effect more speedily than by traditional piecing techniques.*

LEFT: *A man's 'big shirt' in all its splendour, dating from the 1930s. Plain versions began to be worn around 1900 but were superseded by more elaborate patchwork versions in 1915. The narrow stripes of this shirt are pieced, and the whole loose, cool garment is made with typical Seminole perfectionism.*

SEMINOLE INDIAN CUSHION

As bright and simple as children's building blocks, yet with all the jewel-like complexity and sophistication of Roman mosaic, Seminole patchwork is quite unique. Put together from a confetti of cotton pieces joined in kaleidoscopic bands, the design is crisp and the colour singing. But fear not — it is also fun to do, and quicker and easier than its lapidary richness suggests.

SEMINOLE INDIANS IN their rainbow regalia are a magnificent sight — men and women wear intricate patchwork clothes for everyday work as well as the great feast days celebrating spring and autumn. The women wear long and very full skirts composed of five rows of kaleidoscopic pieced cotton, and strings of bead necklaces, weighing up to 25 lb (11 kg), without which they simply do not feel dressed. They used to brush their long black hair over cardboard shapes like lopsided hat-brims, making a strange but elegant asymmetrical halo, but this practice is less common nowadays. The men are resplendent in brilliant overshirts with silk scarves at their necks, and the children wear diminutive versions of their parents' outfits.

Seminole patchwork is made for the sewing machine — its crisp regularity simply could not be achieved any other way. And with a machine, the complex

bands of syncopated colour can be assembled with surprising speed once the basic principle is mastered. As a result, the women take great care of their trusty hand or treadle sewing machines, and many are in faultless working order after fifty years of hard wear, despite the ravages of humidity and the absence of spare parts and repairmen.

The most startling aspect of these exuberant clothes is their raw colour — scarlet, shocking pink, lime green and buttercup yellow are all put together with visual dexterity, while calming doses of black and white combine to produce a result which is exciting and eye-catching but miraculously not brash.

The punctilious workmanship of the tiny pieces of cloth and the careful balancing of colour give these dazzling psychedelic garments a style that could almost be called tasteful, certainly cheerful.

SHOPPING LIST

Plain cotton material 45 in/
115 cm wide:

Scarlet ¼ yd/25 cm

Wine red ¼ yd/25 cm

Green ¼ yd/25 cm

Yellow ¼ yd/25 cm

Off-white ¼ yd/25 cm

Pink (also for piping) ½ yd/45 cm

Black (also for back) ½ yd/45 cm

Piping cord no. 4 (4 mm
diameter): 2¼ yd/2 m 5 cm

Black zip: 14 in/35 cm

18 in/46 cm feather-filled cushion
pad or loose stuffing

THE PALETTE
*Plain scarlet, pink, off-white, yellow, green,
wine red and black.*

THE COMPONENTS

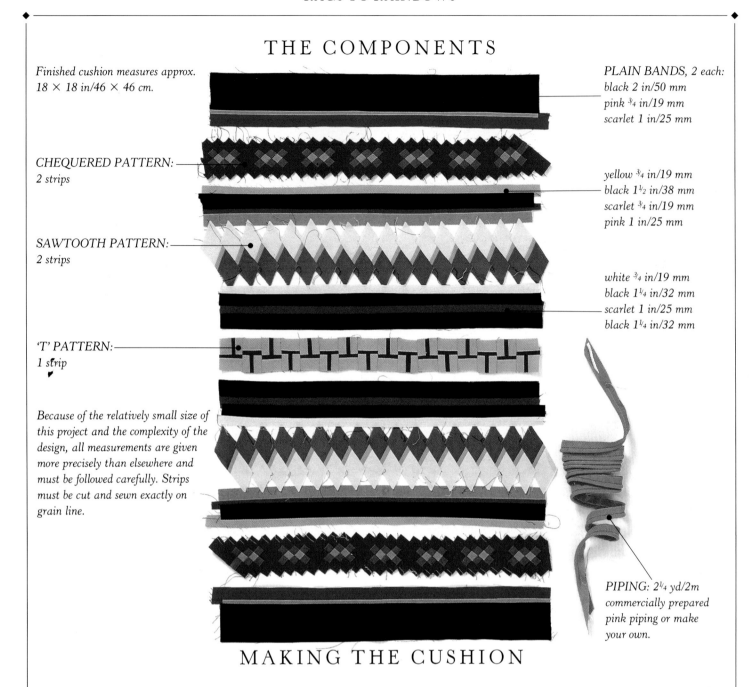

Finished cushion measures approx.
18 × 18 in/46 × 46 cm.

PLAIN BANDS, *2 each:*
black 2 in/50 mm
pink ³/₄ in/19 mm
scarlet 1 in/25 mm

CHEQUERED PATTERN:
2 strips

yellow ³/₄ in/19 mm
black 1¹/₂ in/38 mm
scarlet ³/₄ in/19 mm
pink 1 in/25 mm

SAWTOOTH PATTERN:
2 strips

white ³/₄ in/19 mm
black 1¹/₄ in/32 mm
scarlet 1 in/25 mm
black 1¹/₄ in/32 mm

'T' PATTERN:
1 strip

Because of the relatively small size of this project and the complexity of the design, all measurements are given more precisely than elsewhere and must be followed carefully. Strips must be cut and sewn exactly on grain line.

PIPING: *2¹/₄ yd/2m commercially prepared pink piping or make your own.*

MAKING THE CUSHION

1 For the first Seminole pattern, cut strips at least 30 in/76 cm long: 3 1 in/25 mm wide wine red; 3 1 in/25 mm wide green; 1 1 in/25 mm wide pink; 1 2 in/50 mm wide wine red.

2 Sew together accurately to make 2 strips as shown. Steam press in direction that causes least bulk. Each strip should finish 3 in/75 mm wide. Cut strips into pieces 1 in/25 mm wide.

3 Arrange pieces as shown (if you have not been consistent in using a ¹/₄ in/6 mm seam they will not align). Sew pieces together to make a strip 40 in/102 cm long. Cut to make 2 20 in/51 cm strips. Press.

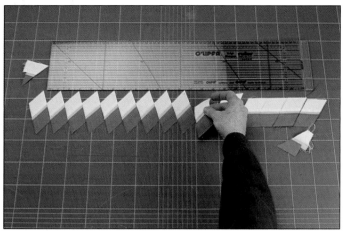

4 Cut 1 strip each of following 36 in/90 cm long: 1½ in/38 mm wide white; ¾ in/19mm wide yellow; 1½ in/38 mm wide green. Sew together and cut into 1½ in/38 mm pieces at a 60° angle.

5 Arrange a zig-zag pattern. Left side of each white diamond should line up with next yellow stripe. Sew together to form a 40 in/ 102 cm strip. Cut to make 2 20 in/51 cm strips. Press as before.

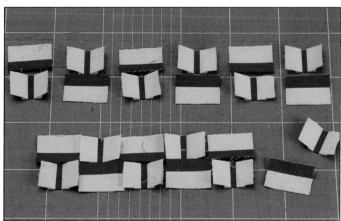

6 Cut strips 30 in/76 cm long: 3 1 in/25 mm wide yellow; 2 ¾ in/19 mm wide wine red. Sew together as shown. Cut strips with central stripe 1 in/25 mm wide; and others 1¾ in/45 mm wide.

7 Sew a strip of 16 Ts as shown. Cut 20 in/51 cm long strips for spacer bands, 2 of each colour (see exploded diagram of components for list of colours and width measurements).

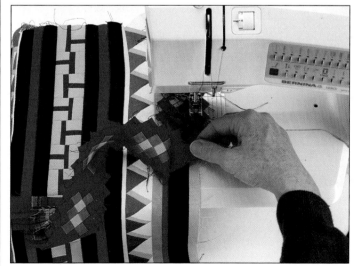

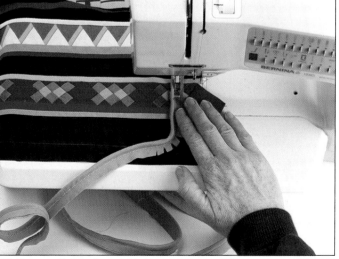

8 Sew strips together, then sew to decorative bands exactly through points of red and zig-zag designs. Draw sewing line on back with water-erasable pen to match seam allowance on plain strip. Tack before sewing to ensure accuracy.

9 Press well. Mark an 18 in/46 cm square with water-erasable pen and sew on prepared piping using a zipper foot. Cut a 20 in/51 cm square of black for back. Sew it to front leaving an opening. Turn right side out, insert pad or stuffing and sew up opening.

SWEDISH WOOLLEN QUILT

INTER LOOMS LARGE in Scandinavian countries. To cheer the months of cold and dark, horseback riders celebrate St Stephen's night under the stars, songs are sung at Christmas, and beautifully painted wooden churches are the focus of music, lights and pealing bells. Christmas cards spring to life, and transport across the snow is by jingling sleigh and reindeer.

The traditional log cabin was entirely constructed of wood, of comforting and insulating thickness. Beds in the large main room were boxed into the wall with a curtain for draught-exclusion and privacy. The wealthy had canopied four-poster beds hung with embroidered curtains. Within this tiny, cosy refuge, winter warmth came from layers of bedding — great thick comforters or down-filled duvets, and patched and pieced quilts. Puffy duvets were covered with striped woollen ticking, attractively bold and bright.

Patchwork designs in varying degrees of splendour were patiently stitched to make a warm splash of colour in the predominantly brown interiors. The tradition stretches back to the fourteenth century and probably beyond. The oldest remaining piece of Swedish patchwork found at Katzenberg, Hessen, dates from 1303. Heraldic textiles featured dramatic appliqué on banners, canopies and wall-hangings, a grand precedent which gradually transmuted into cushions made from bright felted wool cut into geometric shapes.

The nineteenth century bourgeois fashion was for pieced quilts with a passing similarity to British work of the time. Diamonds, hexagons and lozenges of paper-backed silk and cotton were sewn in all-over designs, simply quilted in diamonds. Occasionally, an ambitious needlewoman might add a wide plain border and quilt it with an intricate pattern based on plant shapes.

Wholecloth quilting in wool, silk or linen was a country tradition, with a repertoire of abstract whorls, like Celtic sun signs, swags, flowers and shells, minutely worked. Best of all are the confident multi-coloured pieced strippies, the variants on log cabin, and the unique geometric wedding quilts to be found around Roslagen.

RIGHT: *A bold combination of patterns and pieces in a Swedish country quilt made at the turn of the century from a mixed bag of silks and cottons. The lively partnership of triangular blocks and pieced strips is typical of Roslagen.*

BELOW: *A brave sunburst medallion made from a variety of furnishing fabric samples around 1914 in Norrtälje. Apart from the central star, the quilt is composed entirely of the most basic components — just squares and rectangles.*

LEFT: *Swedish quilters have a unique repertoire for wedding quilts, incorporating all kinds of unusual bits and pieces, including shawls and weddings caps. This strong design was made in Odenslund in 1907. The quilted centre is made from a silk shawl following the local tradition, the rest is tied.*

SWEDISH WOOLLEN QUILT

A wonderful unabashed mixture of woollen checks, stripes, plains, paisleys and florals in a quilt that comes straight from Roslagen on the Stockholm coast. The warm autumnal colours of earth, berries and fruit in this rich combination of patterns make a quilt that is the ultimate in comforting cosiness on winter nights, guaranteed to cheer the chilliest box-bed.

A S IS OFTEN the case, the countrified quilts of Sweden have an ebullience of colour and design lost by their more sophisticated urban counterparts. Pieced quilts in silk, wool or thick cotton come in a vibrant mixture of pattern and colour, usually with plenty of glowing red. There are simple but effective variants on nine-patch with neat diamond borders, scrap strips and windmills combined in a glorious motley of floral and checked fabric, strippy quilts with wide clam-shell quilted borders, wonderful log cabin quilts with wide and sometimes strip-worked borders. Often the borders are given particular attention and may be intricately quilted or carefully pieced from contrasting blocks, or may make a rich dark frame using a more precious fabric than the rest.

Peculiar to Scandinavia are wedding quilts appliquéd with silk caps or put together from silk shawls brought home by seafaring fiancés. In boldness of design these quilts have no equal. Whole shawls or smaller sections are the basis and usually form the centre, surrounded by wide pieced borders in chevrons or

--- SHOPPING LIST ---

Viyella (wool and cotton blend) checks, prints and plains 45 in/ 115 cm wide:

5 different dark tones ¼ yd/25 cm each

4 different light tones ¼ yd/25 cm each

Paisley (border): 1 yd/90 cm

Dark green (binding): ½ yd/45 cm

Viyella (backing): 1⅔ yd/1 m 50 cm

Wool domette (interlining): 1⅔ yd/1 m 50 cm

Cotton thread to match binding

rectangles. The colours are unusual — black and mauve in startling conjunction, or dark green, red and pink paisley in large blocks. Sometimes ribbons are incorporated in the design. Since shawls tend to be square, wedding quilts may be given a wide pieced edging top and bottom to make a rectangle. Precious chintz made the occasional appearance and, as elsewhere, small pieces were eked out by cunning piecing. In Sweden the most appealing treatment was also the simplest — just a rectangle of chintz with a plain border almost as wide.

The wadding, wool or cotton, was usually very heavy, and the quilting generally on the simple side. Quilting is not necessarily continuous, and borders may be decorated with separate leaf and flower shapes stitched at quite widely spaced intervals. Knotting, alone or in combination with quilting, is common. Some quilts have an unusual feature in that the wadding is held captive by ties which are fluffed out into fat pompoms on the back — a bright yellow quilt back, for example, may be resplendent with vibrant blue ties.

THE PALETTE
Six light- and dark-toned checks and prints, one paisley print, plus plain dark navy, dark green, lemon and off-white

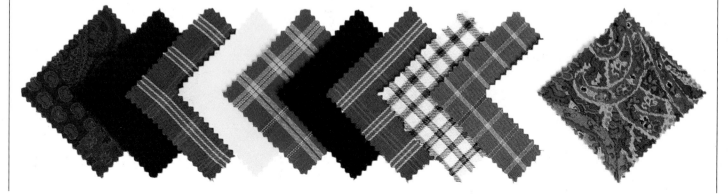

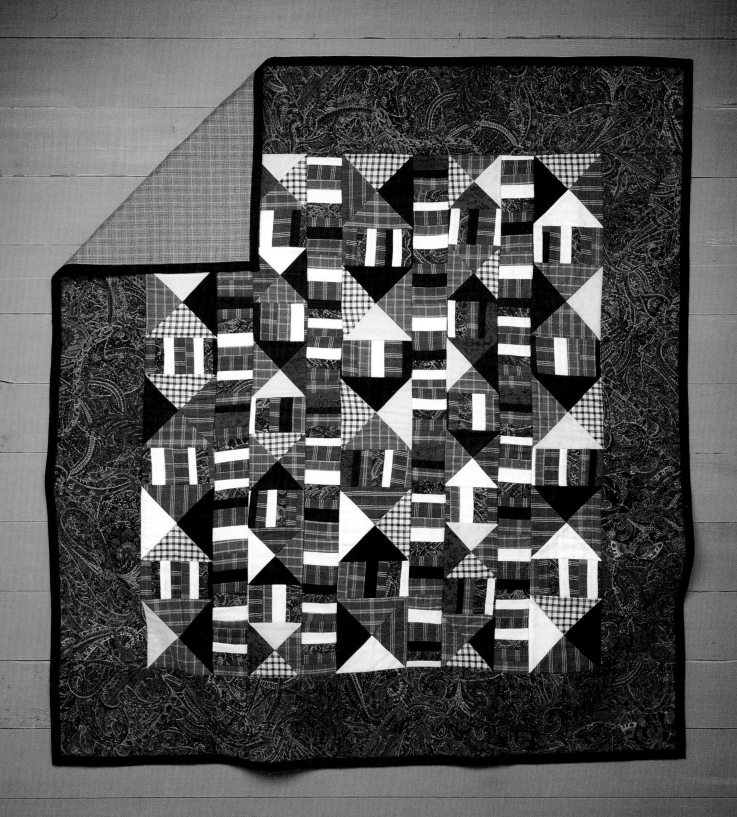

THE COMPONENTS

Use RIT square
templates on
page 124.

*LARGE
HOURGLASS
PATCH
SQUARES:
15 large no. 3
RIT squares in
assorted light
and dark
fabrics.*

*SMALL
HOURGLASS
PATCH
SQUARES:
12 small no. 3
RIT squares in
assorted light
and dark
fabrics.*

*STRIPED
STRIPS: Bands
of strips of
varying widths
in assorted light
and dark
fabrics.*

*BORDER:
4 strips paisley
print approx.
8½ in/22 cm
wide (join where
necessary), cut
to size (top and
bottom pieces to
extend over side
pieces).*

Finished quilt measures approx. 52 × 56 in/132 × 142 cm.

*BINDING:
Dark green
strips 3 in/
75 mm wide.
Join and
prepare as on
page 126.*

MAKING THE QUILT

1 *Using larger template on page 124,
make 15 no. 3 RIT squares, following
step 1 for American Windmill Quilt on
page 30.*

2 *Cut pieces on all drawn lines. Open
and press seams to one side.*

3 *Shuffle resulting large triangular pieces
and join to form squares, making sure no
adjacent pieces are same. Repeat with
smaller template (12 squares). Press.*

4 *To make striped sections, cut strips of random width (1 in/25 mm to 2¼ in/ 60 mm) from remaining materials.*

5 *Sew random strips together lengthways until piece measures about 24 in/60 cm long. Press so that all seams lie in same direction.*

6 *Cut into strips 3½ in/90 mm wide with Olfa cutter.*

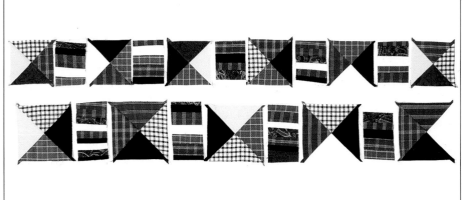

7 *Cut 12 pieces same length as larger squares and 10 pieces same length as smaller. Place between patched squares as shown and sew together to make 3 wide and 2 narrow bands. Make 4 striped strips the length of bands, joining them if necessary. Join bands of squares and striped strips together as in exploded view. Press.*

8 *Cut paisley border 8½ in/21.5 cm wide and sew to quilt (see step 8 for Amish Cot Quilt on page 37). Press. Fix top to domette and backing (see page 125).*

9 *Thread needle and wind bobbin to match front and back. Stitch along all seam lines between rows and around border on flatter side of each seam (see page 125).*

10 *Zig-zag around edge of border and trim excess.*

11 *Cut binding 3 in/75 mm wide and attach to quilt (see page 126).*

TEMPLATES & MAKING-UP INSTRUCTIONS

HAWAIIAN APPLIQUÉ WALL-HANGING
The design is reproduced here at ¼ the actual size. To make
the full-size template, either use the enlarger facility on a photocopier,
or trace the design on to graph paper and copy it on to another,
larger piece of paper, squared up on a scale of 1:4.

BRITISH STRIPPY QUILT
To make the stencil, trace this section (right) on to tracing paper four times so that each half mirrors the other. Lay a piece of acetate on top and cut a channel ⅛ in/ 3 mm wide with a scalpel, leaving lots of bridges.

JAPANESE SASHIKO CUSHION
To make the circular chrysanthemum shape, trace this segment 12 times on to a piece of stiff card.

PANAMANIAN MOLA WALL-HANGING
The three elements are reproduced actual size, so trace the shapes directly on to stiff card.

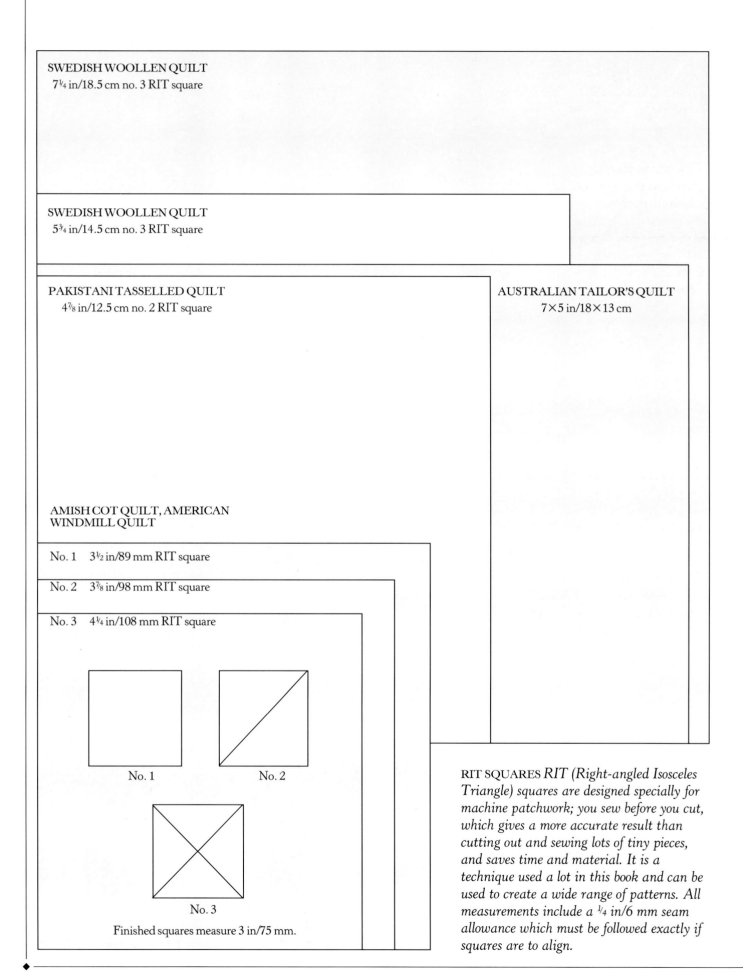

SWEDISH WOOLLEN QUILT
7¼ in/18.5 cm no. 3 RIT square

SWEDISH WOOLLEN QUILT
5¾ in/14.5 cm no. 3 RIT square

PAKISTANI TASSELLED QUILT
4⅞ in/12.5 cm no. 2 RIT square

AUSTRALIAN TAILOR'S QUILT
7×5 in/18×13 cm

AMISH COT QUILT, AMERICAN
WINDMILL QUILT

No. 1   3½ in/89 mm RIT square

No. 2   3⅞ in/98 mm RIT square

No. 3   4¼ in/108 mm RIT square

No. 1   No. 2

No. 3

Finished squares measure 3 in/75 mm.

RIT SQUARES *RIT (Right-angled Isosceles Triangle) squares are designed specially for machine patchwork; you sew before you cut, which gives a more accurate result than cutting out and sewing lots of tiny pieces, and saves time and material. It is a technique used a lot in this book and can be used to create a wide range of patterns. All measurements include a ¼ in/6 mm seam allowance which must be followed exactly if squares are to align.*

STICKY WADDING

Instead of tacking the quilt top, interlining and backing together before quilting, it is quicker and easier to sandwich the layers together with spray adhesive.

1 Cut wadding and backing slightly larger than quilt top. Lay wadding on large plastic sheet on floor and mark into quarters with two pieces of thread stretched across centre. Iron backing smooth and fold in half twice, once across then once lengthwise. Spray wadding generously with adhesive (a large quilt requires a whole 12 oz/ 400 ml can).

2 Carefully line up folds to thread lines and unfold backing on to wadding, smoothing to avoid wrinkles. Turn over and repeat with quilt top. Zig-zag around edge to secure top to wadding and backing and trim excess.

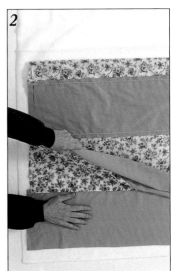

QUILTING STRAIGHT LINES

Thread needle to match quilt top, or use invisible nylon thread if quilting over several different colours. Wind bobbin with thread to match backing fabric.

For best results, use a walking foot attachment, which feeds both top and bottom fabric under the needle and prevents it from slipping. Set stitch length to $3/32$ in/ 2.5 mm (10 stitches to 1 in/ 4 to 1 cm).

Plan your 'route' around the quilt so that it involves as few stops and starts as possible — you don't want to have to sew in too many loose ends. If quilting along seam lines, all seams should have been pressed to lie to one side, rather than open, so that one side is higher than the other.

As you quilt along these lines, the needle should just rub the higher side of the seam (i.e. 'stitch in the ditch'). If quilting straight lines on an unseamed piece of fabric, either draw quilting lines on to the material with a water-erasable pen (e.g. Irish Chain Quilt) or use the printed pattern as a guide (e.g. French Boutis Quilt).

Work at a table large enough to support the full weight of the quilt and when working on the centre of the quilt, roll up the excess to sit under the arm of the machine and secure with bicycle clips. Sew in any loose ends and, if necessary, spray quilt finely with water to remove traces of ink (follow manufacturer's directions).

QUILTING PATTERNS

Draw/trace/stencil design on to the quilt top with water-erasable pen. Replace presser foot with darning foot and lower the feed dog. Use no. 11 needle and, if possible, set machine to run at half-speed and to stop with needle in down position.

Thread needle to match quilt top and wind bobbin to match back. Work at a table large enough to support the full weight of the quilt.

Grip quilt with right hand and guide material under needle with left (wearing rubber gloves will improve your grip). Keep the movement smooth, so that the stitch length is constant (12 stitches to 1 in/5 to 1 cm) and the curves even. Think of the needle as a stationary pen 'drawing' lines on the quilt as you move the material under it.

Check every now and then that backing and wadding are still in line and tack firmly in place if there is any sign of puckering. Sew in loose ends and spray quilt finely with water to remove traces of ink (follow manufacturer's directions).

APPLYING A BINDING

1 Working on wrong side of quilt, start sewing on binding half-way along one side, leaving the first 2–3 in/ 50–75 mm unstitched. Using straight stitch, sew along the fold line of the binding with the raw edge of the binding to the edge of the quilt. At corners, fold binding diagonally through exactly 45°. Press with fingers and mark fold line with pins.

2 Sew up to pin line, then backstitch over a few stitches and release needle.

3 Remove pins and refold on diagonal line.

4 Swing the binding round and start sewing along next side of quilt, still on fold line of binding. Repeat for all corners.

5 On reaching starting point, fold back first raw end and lay new raw end on top. Continue sewing until binding has been attached all round quilt.

6 Turn quilt over and work on right side. Fold binding so folded edge exactly meets line of stitching. Catch down folded edge with tiny zig-zag stitches.

7 At corners fold binding as shown, gently guiding it in place with a pin.

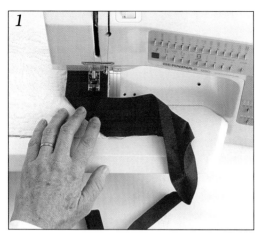

If you are not using a commercially prepared binding, you will need to make your own. Cut enough strips to go round quilt and join along the grain of the fabric — for most bindings the strips should be 3 in/75 mm wide. Fold in half, fold edges to centre and press. Before attaching binding, zig-zag around quilt top to secure interlining and backing, and trim excess.

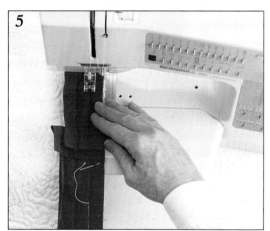

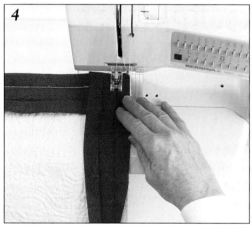

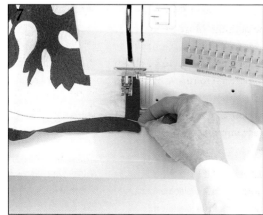

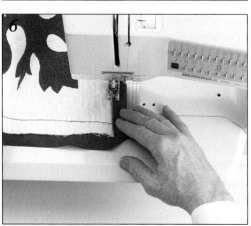

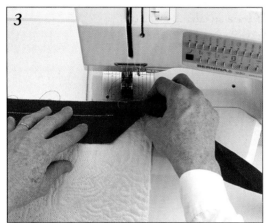

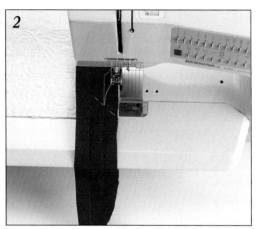

MAKING TASSELS

1 Wind thick, soft embroidery cotton around strip of thick card 2½ in/65 mm wide. Secure tightly at one end with another piece of cotton tied in a knot.

2 Slip tassel off card and cut through loops.

3 Wrap gold thread tightly around base of tassel and sew in ends.

4 Using fine crochet hook, tease strands to make tassels fluffy. Repeat for other 3 tassels and attach to corners of quilt.

EQUIPMENT

The following are required for most of the projects in this book:

ELECTRIC SEWING MACHINE
Should lock stitches correctly on front and back of work; tension easily adjustable. Should be easy to thread, easy to service, with a quick-release lever for presser foot. Walking foot attachment is good investment for straight-line quilting. Must be able to lower feed dog for freehand stitching and useful to be able to set machine to run at half-speed and to stop with needle in down position. Should have long arm to accommodate rolled up quilt while working.

OLFA CUTTER
Rotating blade. Use for cutting long strips, bindings, etc.

SCALPEL
Use for finer, more delicate cutting.

SELF-HEALING MAT
Rubber surface keeps blades sharp, stops material slipping and is printed with grid for accurate cutting.

QUILTER'S RULE
Wide clear plastic rule.

ACETATE
To make quilting stencils or templates. Draw on it with non-water-based marker. Available from art shops.

BONDAWEB
Paper-backed heat-activated adhesive material. Use for machine appliqué. Available 20 in/50 cm wide.

VILENE
Iron-on interfacing.

SPRAY ADHESIVE
Use to bond quilt to wadding and backing. From art shops.

WATER-ERASABLE PEN
Use to draw quilting lines. After quilting, spray with water to remove (follow manufacturer's directions).

WHITE FABRIC MARKER/ TAILOR'S CHALK
Use on darker fabrics, and brush off after quilting.

MASKING TAPE
To mark straight quilting lines.

OTHER:
Stiff card/paper, fine crochet hook, long needle, bulldog clips.

The following ready-made templates are available:

LASER-CUT QUILTING TEMPLATES
Pre-cut stencil patterns (British Strippy Quilt; original quilting designs cut to order). Enquiries to Mrs Paddy Vickery, 1 West End Grove, Farnham, Surrey GU9 7EG.

RIT SQUARE TEMPLATES
Three stiff plastic templates with instructions for making Amish, Windmill and other machine patchwork designs. Available by mail order from Tina Ealovega, c/o Collins and Brown, Mercury House, 195 Knightsbridge, London SW7 1RE, price fixed at £5.00 per pack, including p&p, until December 1993.

GLOSSARY OF ENGLISH/ AMERICAN TERMS

Bondaweb — Stacey Stitch-Witchery.
Calico — White/unbleached cotton with no printed design.
Cotton bump — Brushed cotton flannel, as in a sheet-blanket used in summer.
Lawn — Shirting, usually white or tone on tone, NOT sheer cotton/muslin.
Patchwork — Pieced.
Terylene — Polyester.
Vilene — Iron-on interfacing.
Wadding — Batting.
Winceyette — Brushed cotton.
Wool domette —Wool flannel.

ACKNOWLEDGEMENTS

The illustrations are reproduced by kind permission of the following: *Barbro Ager-Ländin*, Sweden 21 (bottom), 116, 117 (top and bottom); *American Museum in Britain*, Bath 74, 75; *Australian National Gallery* 44; *Beamish Open Air Museum*, County Durham 6, 56 (left), 57 (top), 80; *British Museum*, by courtesy of the Trustees 111 (top); *Crane Gallery/Museum of English Naive Art* 7, 27 (top), 32, 33 (top); *Dundee Art Galleries and Museums* 51 (top left); *Éditions Jeanne Laffitte*, Marseilles 69 (left); *Marilyn Garrow* (photographed by Geoff Dann) 13 (top and bottom); *Joss Graham Oriental Textiles*, London 10 (left), 11 (bottom), 14, 15 (top and bottom), 38 (right), 39 (bottom), 99 (bottom left and right); *Miranda Innes* (photographed by Geoff Dann) 8, 12 (bottom), 98, 99 (top); *Japan Folk Crafts Museum* 86, 87 (top and bottom), 92 (left and right), 93; *Susan Jenkins Antique American Quilts*, London 9 (right), 20, 21 (top), 33 (bottom), 81 (bottom); *Museum of Applied Arts and Sciences*, Sydney, Australia, by courtesy of the Trustees 45 (bottom left and right); *Museum of Fine Arts*, Boston 10/11; *National Library of Australia* 45 (top); *National Trust of Australia* (Victoria) 51 (bottom); *Nederlands Openluchtmuseum* 68, 69 (right); *'Out of the Ark'* (photographed by Ling Wong) 26, 52 (top right), 56 (right); *Peabody Museum of Archaeology and Ethnology*, Harvard University 110, 111 (bottom); *Doris Rau* 38 (left), 39 (top); *Royal Ontario Museum* 9 (left), 62, 63 (top and bottom); *'Tobias and the Angel'* (photographed by Geoff Dann) 57 (bottom); *Tokyo National Museum* 12 (top); *Ulster Folk and Transport Museum* 27 (bottom left and right), 50, 81 (top); *Galerie Urubamba*, Paris (photographed by Geoff Dann) 104, 105 (top left and right × 2, and bottom).

African pieced quilt and Japanese sashiko cushion made by Karin Round.

Templates drawn by Fred Ford and Mike Pilley, Radius.

Many people all over the world have helped in the making of this book, most of all Tina Ealovega, who kept a cool head, pursued every idea with flair and passionate enthusiasm, and found time in a busy life to stitch remorselessly and beautifully. Mrs Paddy Vickery designed the stencil pattern for our British Strippy Quilt. Karin Round helped with the sewing and kindly talked to any Swedish contacts. Of these, Barbro Ager-Ländin was extremely helpful – she is writing her own history of Swedish quilts which will be essential reading. Janet Rae was very helpful and provided essential information, as did Dorothy Daniels of the Quilter's Guild. Gill Turley very kindly took me the time to show me a video from a Swedish quilt exhibition. Joss Graham was extremely generous with information and pictures. Jennifer Pretor-Pinney of the Crane Gallery was very helpful, and Susan Jenkins of the Quilt Museum was absurdly generous with time, information and pictures. Jonathan King at the Museum of Mankind kindly unearthed essential and abstruse details about the Seminole. 'Out of the Ark' and Marilyn Garrow lent us quilts for photography. Jilly Sutton and Irene Bow dyed the Japanese indigo.

At Collins and Brown, Roger Bristow and Carol McCleeve made the book look good, and Sarah Bloxham kept a beady eye and a serene smile about her at all times. Carter Houck is to be thanked for her many useful suggestions.

Finally, vital to this book was the kindly loan of a Bernina 1230 from the Bogod Sewing Machine Company, 50–52 Great Sutton Street, London EC1 (Keith Bassett, 071-253 1198).

Without the following fascinating and truly inspirational books, this one would never have been written: *African Textiles* John Picton and John Mack (BMP); *The Amish Quilt* Eve Wheatcroft Granick (Good Books); *Amish Quilts* Robert Bishop and Elizabeth Safanda (Laurence King); *Anonymous Was a Woman* Mirra Bank (St Martin's Press); *The Art of the Loom* Ann Hecht (BMP); *Clues in the Calico* Barbara Brackman (EPM Publications Inc.); *En Jupon Piqué et Robe D'Indienne* Michel Biehn (Éditions Jeanne Laffitte); *Japanese Decorative Art* Martin Fedderson (Faber and Faber); *Japanese Detail, Traditional Costume and Fashion* Sadao Hibi (Thames and Hudson); *Japanese Quilts* Jill Liddell and Yuko Watanabe (Studio Vista); *Mennonite Quilts and Pieces* Judy Schroeder Tomlonson (Good Books); *The Mingei* Nihon Mingei Kyokai; *Mingei Japanese Folk Art* Robert Moes (The Brooklyn Museum); *Mingei, The Living Tradition in Japanese Arts* (Japan Folk Crafts Museum); *Mola Designs* Frederick W. Shaffer (Dover Design Library); *Nigerian Handcrafted Textiles* Joanne Bubolz Eicher (University of Ife Press); *Patchwork* Pamela Clabburn (Shire Books); *Patchwork Quilts in Australia* Margaret Rolfe (Greenhouse Publications); *Pieced Quilts of Ontario* Dorothy Burnham (Royal Ontario Museum); *Polynesian Barkcloth* Simon Kooijman (Shire Ethnography); *Quilts* Susan Jenkins and Linda Seward (HarperCollins); *Quilts* Judy Wentworth (Crescent Books); *The Quilter's Catalog* Vicki Brooks and Linda Stokes (Main Street); *Sashiko Quilting* Kimi Ota; *Seminole Patchwork* M. Brandebourg (Batsford Press); *Textile Collections of the World* Cecil Lubell; *Textiles of the Kuna Indians of Panama* Herta Puls (Shire Ethnography); *Tifaifai and Quilts of Polynesia* Joyce D. Hammond (University of Hawaii Press); *Traditional Indian Textiles* John Gillow and Nicholas Barnard (Thames and Hudson).